ELIZABETH FARRELL

and the History of Special Education
2nd Edition

Kimberly Kode

Council for Exceptional Children

Council for Exceptional Children
2900 Crystal Drive, Suite 100
Arlington, VA 22202
www.cec.sped.org

Library of Congress Cataloging-in-Publication data

Kode, Kimberly
Elizabeth Farrell and the history of special education / by Kimberly Kode
p. cm.
Includes biographical references.

ISBN 978-0-86586-523-5 (soft cover edition)
ISBN 978-0-86586-525-9 (eBook edition)

CEC Product No. P6234 (soft cover edition)

Design by Tom Karabatakis, TomPromo Marketing.

Printed in the United States of America by Sheridan Books, Inc.

Second edition

10 9 8 7 6 5 4 3 2 1

On August 10, 1922, eighteen students at Teachers College in the summer session decided that the next step in special education was fellowship, that they ought to get together, and know what the other is doing. This International Council … is vigorous and strong: it is to be reckoned with in educational programs in this country.

When you hear of ability groupings, you can look back to a small group of people who, before the term was in general use, were talking about the desirability of teaching children what they could learn, developing their powers, instead of emphasizing their deficiencies. We did that … before any school group had ever dreamed of it.

Now, my last work. The jails are full of your failures—all of you. Your state didn't ask you to be a teacher. You came and offered yourself as a teacher. And I want to challenge the right of any person to be a teacher of another unless that person will exhaust every resource to be a better and better teacher. If these men in jail—and the women, too—had had the kind of teachers that this government expected them to have, I question whether the jails would be full. I am aware that there is subnormality, psychotic conditions, poverty, and what not. But one of the greatest reasons is the lack of right educational opportunity.

I want every teacher here to think now of her failures, of the men and the women whose lives were cut short in their opportunity, because we were not well-trained enough, because the science of education was not an instrument in our hands. How many people are less than they should be because we lack the artistry of creating interest, because we lack the artistry of making attractive the knowledge of the world?

As we consecrate again, this moment, our lives to the education of this country, let us say with Wells "It is a race between destruction and education." I am a teacher, and destruction shall never win.

- Elizabeth E. Farrell
(1930)

Contents

Preface to the Second Edition

My work detailing Elizabeth Farrell's life and professional accomplishments was, in many ways, the result of a happy accident. I was highly interested in basing my historical dissertation on a woman in the field of education, recognizing that despite all the years I had spent as a teacher surrounded primarily by other women, few were sufficiently credited for their work in the field. I came across one line in a special education text that made note of Farrell and realized in short order that I had no idea who she was. That insight sent me down a research "rabbit hole" from which I have not yet emerged.

The more digging I did, the more shocked I became that Elizabeth Farrell was not more well known and the more fearful I became that I was "missing" something—that somewhere out there was a seminal work on Farrell that I had just not yet discovered. It took some time and a lot of research to come to conclusion that nothing had ever been published describing the breadth and depth of Farrell's work, and that it was up to me to do so. Researching Elizabeth Farrell, learning about her, writing about her, and meeting her surviving family members has proven to be one of the most pivotal periods of my life, and I am pleased to say that I am not yet done. There is still much more to be said about Elizabeth Farrell and her esteemed colleagues.

My 2001 dissertation provided the basis for the first edition of this book, published by the Council for Exceptional Children in 2002. As part of the historical research required for my dissertation, I relied extensively on both primary and secondary documents. I was lucky enough to find Elizabeth Farrell's voice in a variety of primary documents, most notably the *Annual Reports of the City Superintendent of Schools to the New York City Board of Education* from 1906 to 1932. Reading these yearly reports, I was able to follow the growth and development of Elizabeth Farrell's foundational work in special education.

Other primary documents included personal correspondence and excerpts from the journal *Ungraded*, published by the Ungraded Classroom Teachers Association and edited by Elizabeth Farrell. I also delved into secondary sources surrounding the work of Lillian Wald and the Henry Street Settlement; records from New York University, Teachers College at Columbia University, and the State University of New York at Oswego; city census records and newspaper accounts; and, of course, other information related to the history of special education.

My goal throughout this experience was to pull together the threads of information obtained from these and other sources to create as rich a work as possible, thereby ensuring that Elizabeth Farrell's name would no longer be a forgotten footnote of history, a name included without fanfare in a special education textbook. Farrell had no way of knowing that her decisions of that time would prove so influential on the special education processes and procedures of today, of course, and I suspect she would have been humbled by the realization of it, but that humility should not stand in the face of the recognition she deserves. I'm proud to have been the person most able to see that achieved.

This second edition includes information from my dissertation that further stands to "round out" the picture of Elizabeth Farrell and her contributions. It is my hope that these additions further cement Elizabeth's name and place in the minds of those who both work and research in the field of special education.

My thanks to Michael Wehmeyer for his contribution to this edition; his Epilogue places Elizabeth's accomplishments in the "big picture" of special education and its development. His remarkable sense of the historical context of her work provides all with a better understanding of its importance, and I am grateful to him for both recognizing it and being gracious enough to write about it.

My sincere thanks also to the Council of Exceptional Children for their continued interest in keeping Elizabeth Farrell's memory alive and part of the collective consciousness of the organization. Just as Farrell did not found the Council alone, neither do any of us who work in special education do so alone, and the CEC continues to recognize the importance of professional fellowship just as Farrell and her colleagues did at its founding in 1922. Beginning then with only 12 members, the fact that the CEC now has over 20,000 members proves the how valued community really is.

I owe a debt to Jackie and John Farrell, Jr., members of Elizabeth Farrell's family, who helped me get to know their Aunt Lizzie and understand the Farrell family history. They have been kind and wonderful throughout this extended adventure, and I am so thankful to them for inviting me into their lives and allowing me to stay. I will forever be grateful to Elizabeth for introducing us.

Finally, a thank you to my own family. My dissertation was completed in 2001, when I was newly married and my family was just beginning. The result of this timing is that my children, Emily and Evan, have known about Elizabeth Farrell their whole lives, and my husband, Scott, has heard about Elizabeth for the entire length of our marriage. It is little wonder they never bother to ask when my work with Elizabeth will be finished.

K.K.

Introduction

History balances the frustration of "how far we have to go" with the satisfaction of "how far we have come." It teaches tolerance for the human shortcomings and imperfections, which are not uniquely of our generation, but of all time.

Lewis F. Powell, Jr.
(as cited in Peter, 1977, p. 247)

Reflecting on the history of education, and, more specifically, the history of special education, it is easy to feel self-satisfied with the improvements in the treatment and education of people with disabilities made over the past 50 years or so. The passage of Public Law 94-142 (the Education of All Handicapped Children Act) and Public Law 101-336 (the Americans with Disabilities Act) at the end of the 20th century served to focus the country and its citizens on the rights and needs of people with disabilities. Reauthorization of these laws (as the Individuals with Disabilities Act and the ADA Amendments Act), combined with landmark court cases since *Brown v. Board of Education* (1954)—such as *PARC v. Commonwealth of Pennsylvania* (1972), *Mills v. Board of Education of the District of Columbia (1972),* and *Hudson v. Rowley* (1982)—did much to ensure that people with disabilities are treated with dignity and respect. Today, the majority of students with disabilities are educated alongside their typically developing peers for most of their school day; the principles of universal design (enabling physical access) have influenced efforts to ensure that these students have equal access to all elements of the educational experience.

However, the groundwork for this inclusive environment was laid years before, often by educators whose names remain anonymous. In fact, the progress that we in the 21st century are so eager to take credit for grew out of social and scientific factors that influenced education in America a century ago. New York City's public school system was a forerunner in the education of students with disabilities, and at its helm was Elizabeth E. Farrell, a first-generation American and schoolteacher. Even today, when so much of school reform originates at the administrative or university level and trickles down to the classroom, New York City is distinct. Its special education program began instead with one classroom in one school taught by one teacher—Elizabeth Farrell. Shaped by her experiences teaching in a one-room schoolhouse in rural New York State, as well as her devotion to the underclass, Farrell created an "ungraded" class based on a program of individualized instruction. Although this was not a unique concept, its originality lay in applying the idea to the education of underachieving children in and by the public schools. Farrell was optimistic enough to believe that

> the largest and most complex school system in the country—
> perhaps the world— with its hundreds of thousands of children,
> its rigid curriculum, its mass methods, could be modified to
> meet the needs of the atypical—often the least lovely and most
> troublesome of its pupils. (Wald, 1941, pp. 134–135)

That one ungraded classroom she created led to many others, building a network of teachers taking up the same cause, and to the establishment of a Department of Ungraded Classes in 1906—with Farrell as its director. As head of this department, Farrell used her influence to change the paradigm of the city school system and its methods, establishing policy and working to professionalize the role of the special education teacher.

The Historical Setting

After centuries of being shunned, abandoned, and mistreated, progress towards fairer treatment for people with disabilities began in the late 18th century, with Jean Itard's efforts to teach the "Wild Boy of Aveyron." This child, who had been seen running naked through the woods in France, was placed under the care of Itard, chief medical officer for the National Institute for the Deaf and Dumb. Believing the boy's condition was curable, Itard worked with him on reading and speaking. After 5 years, the boy, whom the doctor had named Victor, was only able to read and understand a few words, so Itard reluctantly ceased their work.

Other scientists of the time were also becoming interested in the treatment of people with disabilities. Edouard Seguin, who was associated with Itard, immigrated to the United States and worked with Samuel Howe to initiate the establishment of institutional care for people with disabilities. Together, they instated institutional facilities in Massachusetts, Pennsylvania, Ohio, Connecticut, and New York. In the early 1900s, however, attitudes in the United States regarding the treatment of these people took a considerable step backwards. Studies published in the Reconstruction era, like those penned by Richard Dugdale in 1877 and Reverend Oscar McCulloch in 1888, associated disabilities with crime and poverty (Krishef, 1983); in their wake, the role of institutions shifted from protecting those who were "different" from the public to protecting the public from those who were "different."

At the time, many people believed that intellectual and cognitive disabilities were inheritable and feared that evil, crime, and disease would spread if people with disabilities were allowed to procreate.

Indeed, one of America's most esteemed scientists, Henry Herbert Goddard—who was a contemporary of Elizabeth Farrell and a leader at the Vineland Training School for Feeble-minded Boys and Girls in New Jersey—further popularized this notion by concluding that retardation was genetically transmitted and perpetuated in family lines because of "bad blood." Scientists and government officials alike supported the practice of eugenics, a science that traced and manipulated the proliferation of certain genetic factors in order to improve the quality of the human species. At the time, many people believed that intellectual and cognitive disabilities were inheritable and feared that evil, crime, and disease would spread if people with disabilities were allowed to procreate. In 1911, the Research Committee of the Eugenics Section of the American Breeder's Association recommended a practice of lifelong segregation and sterilization so that people with disabilities could not reproduce and thus pass on undesirable traits. Within 50 years, nearly 30,000 people with disabilities in the United States were sterilized (Krishef, 1983, pp. 26–28).

Around the same time, huge waves of desperate people were immigrating to America (Batterberry & Batterberry, 1973). Initially, these immigrants were mostly from western and northern European countries, with significant numbers of English, Irish, Germans, and Norwegians. Later, people from Eastern European countries—Hungary, Poland, and Czechoslovakia—as well as from Italy and Greece joined these, making urban areas such as New York City great melting pots. In fact, by the time the first decade of the 20th century had passed, nearly one seventh of New York City's population was foreign-born (Longstreet, 1975). Although some of these immigrants simply passed through New York to settle elsewhere, many were forced to remain. Lacking in both language and disposable income, a great number found themselves setting up new lives in the shantytowns and slums that mushroomed in various parts of the city. These immigrants, who had sought hope and fortune in America, merely shifted their living quarters from the ghettos in their home countries to similar areas of poverty in urban New York City.

The most notorious slum area in the city was Manhattan's Lower East Side. Millions of people made that corner of New York their first—and sometimes last—stop. This land, located between the Hudson and East Rivers, became one of the most densely populated regions in the United States (Siegel, 1983). Progressive reformer and founder of the Visiting Nurses Service, Lillian Wald, described the conditions there:

> They were packed into dank, airless tenement rooms like ramshackle pieces of furniture in a warehouse. These firetraps they called homes had broken-down stairs, evil-smelling outdoor toilets, rarely a bathtub, and often no running water. The streets … were crammed with shops, pushcarts, and peddlers hawking … bargains…. The hectic commerce was interlaced with piles of rotting garbage, horsedrawn wagons, and fire escapes strewn with household possessions. (Siegel, 1983, p. 25)

Working with Mary Brewster, a like-minded classmate from New York Hospital's School of Nursing, Wald founded one of the first settlement houses in American history, the Henry Street Settlement. Because the Settlement was built on the belief that living and working in the community was the most effective way to improve social conditions, Wald and her colleagues interacted with the Lower East Side immigrant population daily.

One of Wald's main concerns was the education of the children there, and in 1899 she began to hear of a teacher's work at Public School #1, the

Henry Street School. This teacher, as it was reported to Wald by a settlement resident, "had ideas" (Wald, 1915, p. 117). Intrigued, Wald sought an acquaintance with the teacher, Elizabeth Farrell; her "ideas," combined with the support of Wald and the Henry Street Settlement, developed into the first coordinated attempt to educate atypical children.

The ungraded class system that Farrell created became the model for similar educational programs throughout the United States and, later, the basis for our current system of special education. Although most people with a background in special education are familiar with the contributions of men like Goddard, Seguin, Itard, and Howe, with the exception of Montessori, few women's names are well known. It is most certainly not for a lack of involvement of women in the field of education.

The Influence of Elizabeth Farrell

Elizabeth Farrell changed the educational structure of the New York Public School System. Her work laid the foundation for a curriculum designed to address the needs of children with disabilities who were unable to succeed in the typical classroom setting. Her vision for schools was far in advance of the profession at the time, and her philosophies became the basis for special education programs in place in schools all over the United States today.

It was perhaps Farrell's first decision as department head that would prove the most monumental for the future of special education programming and legislative action. After extensive study of Great Britain's approach to identifying and educating students with disabilities, Farrell sought to adopt a similar methodical procedure of examination and record-keeping—but one that was not differentiated by separate programs, separate facilities, and separate schools, believing such a policy would stigmatize and isolate students with special education needs. Her position and empassioned argument for eliminating this type of segregation would later be echoed in the landmark Supreme Court decision *Brown v. Board of Education* (1954), which prohibited the idea of "separate but equal" education.

Farrell also disputed the premise held by many at that time that special class programs were to serve as a precursor to institutional life. The goal of the special class, Farrell believed, was not to prepare students for lives in an institution but to return children back to their original classroom setting after their difficulties had been addressed. Again, this judgment proved pivotal, as it served as the framework for later "mainstreaming" and inclusion efforts in this country.

Similarly, Farrell advocated for a well-rounded assessment of a student's abilities, rather than reliance on intelligence testing as the single measure for placement of a child in the ungraded class. Taking this position meant going up against Henry Herbert Goddard, one of the nation's premier experts on the use of intelligence testing in the schools. Her strong stance on this topic effectively prevented the New York City Board of Education from endorsing Goddard's findings regarding intelligence testing in his 1911–1912 New York School Inquiry report.

Elizabeth Farrell anticipated types of exceptionalities that had not yet been identified, comparing the emerging science of education to the field of medicine:

> There was a time in the evolution of medical science when people fell into two groups—well people and sick people.... The tendency in medical research to make closer classification in order that treatment may be more exact and definite. The application of a method similar to this is what the school needs. (Farrell, 1927, p. 7)

To further this effort, she created the Psycho-Educational Clinic, employing professionals from education, medicine, psychology, and social services, to operate in conjunction with the Department of Ungraded Classes. To this day, a variety of testing and evaluation procedures are required to establish a child's needs for special education services and tailor services to meet those individual needs.

Although not a psychologist herself, she recognized the importance of applied psychology in the schools and sought to build a body of knowledge based on information rather than opinion.

Farrell forever linked the profession of psychology to special education through her work with the New York State Association of Consulting Psychologists (later the New York State Psychological Association). Although not a psychologist herself, she recognized the importance of applied psychology in the schools and sought to build a body of knowledge based on *information* rather than *opinion*. Her union with this professional organization served to increase her credibility and was yet another example of the many ways in which

Farrell promoted collegiality and professional improvement among those that labored in the public school systems.

Despite her hard work creating a model of individualized education, it is uncertain how Farrell would view the current state of special education in this country. No doubt pleased to find that federal law requires accommodations be made for exceptional learners, Farrell might be dismayed by the sheer number of students who need support—many of whom do not qualify for special education services. When she encountered similar conditions in her work with the Psycho-Educational Clinic, Farrell ensured that children who did not qualify for a special class placement still received some degree of support and assistance. She further believed that placement in the ungraded classrooms should occur only after other types of intervention had been exhausted. These principles would serve as precursor to the response to intervention (RTI) approaches that developed decades later. Elements of RTI such as research-based classroom instruction, screening, and progress monitoring—now viewed as essential to providing appropriate intervention in the general education setting—made their tentative debut as part of Farrell's system of ungraded classes.

Unfortunately, Farrell would most likely be disappointed to learn that the educational disparity she sought to rectify in her work as part of the progressive reform movement is still the norm in communities throughout the United States. There are many children who, for reasons related to socio-economics, race, gender, language, school funding issues, and limited opportunities are unable to receive a quality education. Despite her struggle to improve social and educational conditions, the United States is still largely centered around a system of "haves" and "have nots." In many ways, not much has changed.

About This Book

Chapter 1 provides a biography of Elizabeth Farrell's personal life, focusing on her family background, her early life, education, and professional work prior to her arrival in New York City. This chapter also provides information on and the rationale for the establishment of the "ungraded" classes. Chapter 2 presents the challenges Elizabeth Farrell dealt with as the system of ungraded classes evolved, including the influences of eugenics and intelligence testing. Chapter 3 gives special attention to Farrell's work in the area of teacher training and professional development and the formation of the Council for Exceptional Children. It also details the end of her career and her life.

It should be acknowledged that the terminology used by Elizabeth Farrell and others of her time period to refer to individuals with disabilities is significantly different than that currently used and would be considered offensive and inappropriate by today's standards. These terms reflect the times in which Farrell lived, however, and an understanding of them is essential to appreciate her efforts to create the system of specialized education for which she is credited.

It appears as if these terms were "understood" and as a result were not well defined. Many terms were also used interchangeably, further complicating matters. In the historical research, where possible, primary documents have been used to provide definitions. In other instances, working definitions have been created based on the available literature:

- *Atypical* or *atypical children* refers to children who have educational needs that differ or are beyond what is usual for a child in school.

- *Defective, mental defective*, and *mentally deficient* refers to children who, for a variety of reasons, are unable to succeed in the traditional classes in the public school. The term *defective* was used in "lieu of 'ungraded' in some localities because of its vagueness" (Teachers Council Report, 1920). Further, it is a general term used to describe students with "varying degree of mental defect" (Edson, 1921).

- *Feebleminded* or *feeblemindedness* comprises "all degrees of mental defectives due to arrested or imperfect mental development as a result of which the person affected is incapable of competing on equal terms with his normal fellows, or of managing himself or affairs with ordinary prudence" (Teachers Council Report, 1920).

- *Laggard* refers to "the slow child, the child whose development is sluggish, one who, with other things equal, is overage for his grade" (Farrell, 1915).

- *Retarded* refers to the number of years a child is behind in his or her education. For example, a 12-year-old student in the fourth grade would be 2 years retarded. It can also describe a student who is not progressing through the grades.

- *Ungraded* is used to describe "one who presents a problem of special education which cannot be adequately met elsewhere" (Edson, 1921).

- *Ungraded class* or *ungraded classes* refers to a "class of several grades composed of children of low mentality" (Edson, 1921). It describes the organizational structure of special education classes in the New York City public school system. These classes contrast the traditional, age-related graded system employed in school systems.

- *Special class* or *special classes* refer also to this nontraditional system of organization.

We can only speculate as to how special education in the United States would be different were it not for the dedication and labor of Elizabeth E. Farrell. It was her friend and mentor Lillian D. Wald who perhaps stated it best when she reflected upon the importance of Farrell's work:

> Looking back upon the struggles to win formal recognition of the existence of these children ... we realize our colleague's devotion to them, her power to excite enthusiasm in us, and her understanding of the social implications of their existence, came from a deep-lying principle that every human being ... merits respectful consideration of his rights and personality. (Wald, 1915, pp. 120–121).

CHAPTER 1

The Early Years

Over 2.5 million immigrants arrived in America between 1840 and 1850 (Carpenter, 1927, as cited in Yans-McLaughlin & Lightman, 1997, pp. 324–325)—and Elizabeth Farrell's parents were among them. Unlike many immigrants of the time, however, Elizabeth's parents had a head start on their future. Skilled in the textile industry, the Farrell family was able to overcome many of the difficulties that faced strangers in a foreign land and achieve financial security and economic success. Despite these achievements, they could not have foreseen the impact their daughter would later have on the education of millions of children throughout the United States.

Michael Farrell, Elizabeth's father, arrived in America from Kilkenny, Ireland in 1848 when he was 13 years old. The Farrell family settled in Catskill, New York, at the foot of the Catskill Mountains, a village made famous in 1800 by Washington Irving as the scene of Rip Van Winkle's legendary nap. Although what led the Farrell family to settle in Catskill is largely unknown, travel to that region was fairly easy, made so by the establishment of a regular steamboat route in 1838 up the Hudson River from New York City. Further, the water power of the Hudson River combined with the completion of the Susquehanna Turnpike in 1800 led to the development of a variety of industries in the area: tanneries, gristmills, sawmills, papermills, and woolen mills (Adams, 1990, p. 15).

Elizabeth Farrell's mother, Mary Smith, also immigrated to the United States as a child. Born in Wales in 1838, she was the second oldest of six children, with her two youngest siblings born after the family arrived in the United States. Her family settled in Marcellus, New York, a small village in central New York State that served as home to several different woolen mills.

It was probably the mill industry that brought Michael Farrell and Mary Smith together. By 1863 they had married and were living in Marcellus, and Michael Farrell was working in one of the local mills as a wool carder (Marcellus, 1865). The Farrell family moved throughout central New York State as Michael Farrell took positions of increasing responsibility and pay at area mills, eventually settling in Utica, New York. Located on the Mohawk River, Utica's growth as both an industrial and commercial center is attributed to the completion of the Erie Canal in 1825, which enabled establishment of the nation's first large textile steam mill.

The Education of Elizabeth Farrell

Elizabeth Farrell was born in 1870. Growing up in Utica, she was enrolled first at the Hamilton Street School, a primary school, and later at Utica Catholic Academy. An all-girl school founded in 1834, Utica Catholic Academy was run by the Sisters of Charity, a religious order dedicated to nursing the sick, helping the needy, and educating children. Originally known as St. John's Select and Free School, the Academy became tuition-free in 1876.

After the death of Elizabeth's mother in 1885, her father moved the family to Oneida, New York, where he established a knit mill, M. Farrell and Son. Years later, after his son moved on to other enterprises and their operation was dissolved, Michael moved his daughters back to Utica and became president of Central Mills Manufacturing, another knit mill. With his increasing wealth and newfound affluence, Michael Farrell could afford to send Elizabeth to college. After her graduation from Utica Catholic Academy, Elizabeth enrolled at the Oswego Normal and Training School (now the State University of New York at Oswego) to study teaching.

The curriculum at the Oswego Normal and Training School was based on Pestalozzi's "object" method, which proposed a change from the traditional book or lecture method to one where real objects are studied and the connections between school and life are explored. This teaching philosophy would later prove to be the first of many important influences in her professional life. Years later, Farrell discussed how she had reflected on such ideas when creating the curriculum of the ungraded class:

> To Pestalozzi we go to learn that our aim is not that the child should know what he does not know but that he should behave as he does not behave, and the road to right action is right feeling. And again he says: "I have proved that it is not regular work

that stops the development of so many poor children but the turmoil and irregularity of their lives, the privations they endure, the excesses they indulge in when opportunity offers; the wild rebellious passions so seldom restrained; and the hopelessness to which they are so often prey." (Farrell, 1908b, as cited in Sarason & Doris, 1979, pp. 304–305)

After graduating from Oswego's English degree program in 1895, Elizabeth took a position as one of four teachers at the Blandina Street Training School. Blandina's purpose was to train teachers for the State of New York, and its course of instruction was a combination of theory, with classes in educational psychology, school management, education history, and practice, requiring its teacher candidates to substitute teach and have their teaching observed. After 2 years working in teacher training, Elizabeth accepted a position as a teacher in a small community near Utica, where she taught in a one-room schoolhouse; a year later she left to accept a teaching position in New York City, in the Lower East Side of Manhattan.

What compelled Elizabeth to leave the protective enclave her family created in central New York State and move to New York City? The conditions in New York City were certainly a radical departure from the environment in which she grew up. However, Elizabeth's generation was the first sizable generation of American college graduates to come to maturity without clearly defined roles:

This was especially true for many young women who, if they wished to embark on a career, had few other useful activities open to them.... As a result, America had a sizable group of educated women searching for self-satisfaction and a way to play a more important role in society than custom permitted .... The complexity and challenge of the large city, however, offered them opportunities to create meaningful careers for themselves and at the same time rescue society from the social ills resulting from rapid industrialization and urban change. (Trattner, 1999, pp. 171–172)

In addition, there was a trend at the time, an "urge felt by certain middle and upper-class men and women to help make urban life more just, tolerable, and decent ... to apply their knowledge and skills to social problems" (Link & McCormick, 1983, p. 72). Whatever the motive behind Elizabeth's decision, in moving to New York City she found herself in a city in the midst of dramatic change.

Lillian Wald and the Henry Street Settlement

Elizabeth arrived in New York City in 1899, a pivotal time in the city's history; the city recently had been restructured to create a metropolitan area of approximately 306 square miles, comprising the boroughs of Manhattan, the Bronx, Brooklyn, Richmond County, and Long Island, as well as the cities of Newtown, Flushing, Jamaica, and Hempstead in the county of Queens. As a result of this restructuring there was a net increase of approximately 5% of the city's student population, making the City of New York now responsible for the education of almost half a million pupils (Maxwell, 1899, p. 34; Sarason & Doris, 1979, p. 295). This new district saw a need for teachers in parts both comparatively sparse and densely populated—and there was no part of New York City more densely populated than Manhattan's Lower East Side. By 1893, 1.5 million human beings lived in the congested neighborhood of the Lower East Side, "huddled together in cramped tenements" in an area described by observers as "the home of pushcarts, paupers, and consumptives" (Trattner, 1999, p. 164).

Working from a background in nursing, the main focus for Wald and Brewster was the prevention and treatment of health problems, but seeing increasing numbers of neighborhood children missing school due to ill health, their interest in education grew.

At the center of the Lower East Side neighborhood was Henry Street, and at its core was the Henry Street Settlement. Founded by Lillian Wald and her classmate from New York Hospital's School of Nursing, Mary Brewster, the settlement reflected the guiding philosophy behind the progressive reform movement: The most effective way to improve social conditions and public health would come from a social reformer's living and working in the community (United Neighborhood Houses, n.d.). Working from a background in nursing, the main focus for Wald and Brewster was the prevention and treatment of health problems, but seeing increasing numbers of neighborhood children missing school due to ill health, their interest in education grew. Thus, it was inevitable that they "should take a vital interest in the education offered the children of the city throughout the public schools" (Wald, 1941, p. 133), and their involvement in Public School #1, the Henry Street School, became an increasing focus.

The Henry Street School

Founded by the women of the Society of Friends in 1802, the Henry Street School faced a multitude of challenges. In 1899 the Compulsory Education Provision had passed, stating that all children between the ages of 8 and 12 must attend school from October to June and that children between the ages of 12 and 14 could work only if they attended school at least 80 days. This new provision meant that children who earlier had spent their time working or walking the streets would now be forced to attend school. Many schools were not equipped to handle such a large number of students, and by June of that year there were over 2,200 pupils at the Henry Street School, making it so overcrowded that many students were only able to attend part time.

Further, with a student enrollment largely made up of those children that lived within the immediate neighborhood, teachers faced a student population with a variety of needs, many of which were beyond the scope of what they had been trained to deal with. Often these children had several strikes against them before they ever entered the school doors: Some spoke little or no English, some had physical or mental problems that interfered with their learning, and some had only attended school erratically. Unable to meet the instructional and behavioral needs of many of these students, teachers throughout New York City struggled to find a means of coping.

Elizabeth Farrell's situation was no different. Her first class at the Henry Street School "grew out of conditions in a neighborhood furnished in many serious problems in truancy and discipline" (Farrell, 1906–1907, p. 91). In her class of boys between the ages of 8 and 16 years old, most had been unsuccessful in the classes where they had encountered "ordinary means of teaching ... where intellect is appealed to directly requiring of the child the ability to think in the abstract" (Brown, 1905, p. 431). Some were considered incorrigible and unwilling to follow school rules; others were frequently truant; some could neither read nor count; others were several years behind their grade level; and many had health problems that interfered with their school attendance and ability to learn. As Farrell noted, "school, as they found it, had little or nothing for them"; and thus they had "set themselves against what society had organized for their welfare, the educational system" (Farrell, 1925, p. 10).

The paradigm in use in the schools of New York City did little to address students' individual differences or learning problems. Rice's observation (1893) of the teaching of over 1,200 teachers in schools in 36 cities noted that schools "aim to do little, if anything beyond crowding the memory of the child with a certain number of cut-and-dried facts" (pp. 38–39, as cited in Sarason & Doris, 1979, p. 291). In his report, Rice singled out the typical New York City primary school as "a hard, unsympathetic, mechanical-drudgery school, a school in which the light of science has not yet entered. Its characteristic features lie in the severity of discipline, a discipline of enforced silence, immobility, and mental passivity" (Rice, 1893, p. 220, as cited in Sarason & Doris, 1979, p. 291).

Maintaining that education should be based on providing "the child the right education—the kind of training which he needs, therefore which he accepts" (Farrell, 1913–1914), Farrell had some ideas as to how the curriculum could be organized to keep her students interested in school while more fully addressing their needs. Prior to asking the School Board to fund any special instruction districtwide, however, she wanted to develop and monitor the success of one class based on her curricular suppositions. Thus, she began to experiment with the structure and dynamics of her own class.

During this critical period of development, Farrell sought guidance and support from several different sources: her principal, William L. Ettinger; Superintendent William H. Maxwell; Charles Burlingham, president of the Board of Education; and Felix Warburg, a member of both the Board of Education and the Henry Street Settlement. It was under their watchful eyes that Farrell had the freedom to examine various methods of teaching and make decisions regarding what worked best in her classroom with her pupils (Sarason & Doris, 1979). Farrell's curricular model was completely individualized and pragmatic, with complete "freedom from the prescribed course of study" (Stevens, 1903, p. 116). Indeed, she believed in the strength of a curriculum based on the varying needs of each one of her students. Farrell noted she looked forward to the time

> when every teacher will know what the ability of the child is, and the child's burden as it is represented by the course of study he undertakes. That burden will be trimmed to his ability. It will not be the same burden for every child, but it will be a burden for every child commensurate with his ability to bear. (Farrell, 1925, p. 17)

Intended to exploit the potential of multi-age grouping that she had witnessed while teaching in rural New York, Farrell wanted to treat learning in a holistic manner, building on each individual student's experiences. She felt that the students "had to be shown that school could be more than mere study of books in which they had no interest. They had to be convinced that to attend school was a privilege not a punishment" (Farrell, 1906–1907, p. 91). To change this perception, Farrell used a variety of nontraditional supplies to teach the boys in her class:

> Instead of books, they had tin cans; instead of spellers, they had picture puzzles to solve; instead of penmanship lessons, they had watercolor paints and brushes; instead of arithmetic and multiplication tables, they had wood and tools, and things with which to build and make. (Farrell, 1925, p. 11)

She believed these "ungraded" classes needed to "appeal to the constructive, the acquisitive, the imitative instincts in the child" and be "full of things to do, full of interesting activities to pursue, full of constructive activity" (Farrell, 1907, p. 11; Farrell, 1925, p. 11). An observer of her class in 1904 noted that despite the demands of her class of 19 students ranging from ages 6 to 17,

> Each child is studied individually and his education is fitted to his needs. The chief aim is to create in the boys a love of work so that when they go out into the world, they will not join the ranks of the criminal class. For this reason, everything is related to manual training and made subordinate to it. They always have some subject as a center; at present it is the farm.
>
> In woodwork, they are making a house and barn, fences, furniture, and flower-boxes. They are weaving the rugs for the floor, making a hammock, doing raffia work and basketry. They went to the country for the soil to plant their miniature fields, and sent to Washington for seeds. In painting, their subjects have been apple blossoms and violets with an illustrated trip to Bronx Park. In picture study, they have taken "Oxen Plowing," "The Angelus," etc. In arithmetic, the older boys measure in a concrete way, the rooms of the house and the fields. In their written work in English, they are having stories of farm life, and reports of personal observation; in reading, stories of dogs, horses, making hay, and so on; in spelling, words relating to manual occupations, e.g., "soil, seeds, leaves, barn." In nature work, they are studying soils, the earthworm, buds and seeds. This is simply suggestive

of the excellent work that the boys are taking up at present. The subjects are chosen and the different studies related to the center with the purpose of developing the social instincts in the boys. (Chace, 1904, as cited in Sarason & Doris, 1979, p. 301)

Word of Farrell's classroom successes quickly spread throughout the Lower East Side, and Lillian Wald at the Henry Street Settlement began to hear the enthusiastic rumors. Wald sought Farrell's acquaintance, and it wasn't long before Farrell moved into the Settlement House, becoming a trusted friend and ally to Wald for the next 25 years. At the House, Wald surrounded herself with middle-class women with no ties to husbands or children who could fully devote their energies to their work within the Henry Street community, and Farrell fit right in. Years later, Wald described the importance the Settlement House and community had on Farrell's visions for education: "The Settlement's rich understanding of people, life, events, its multicolored and changing activities, provided her with a background which helped keep her own thought and emotion fresh and vital" (Wald, 1941, p. 138).

Years later, Wald described the importance the Settlement House and community had on Farrell's visions for education: "The Settlement's rich understanding of people, life, events, its multicolored and changing activities, provided her with a background which helped keep her own thought and emotion fresh and vital".

Wald encouraged Farrell's work with children and assisted her in refining her theory of special instruction. She helped provide equipment not yet on the School Board's requisition list and is credited with persuading the New York City School Board in 1902 to hire the first school nurse (Coss, 1989, p. xv). Most important, however, Wald worked to interest School Board members and others in Farrell's work.

The Establishment of "Special Classes"

With Wald as her mentor, members of the Board of Superintendents began to take a particular interest in Farrell's program. Before recommending any general rule to establish special instruction for similar atypical children throughout the district, however, the Board thought it best to "experiment in several schools with classes affording various courses of study or other special features" (Maxwell, 1902, p. 109). Maxwell concurred, having earlier recommended that "no very extensive schema be adopted" because "mistakes will certainly be made in any attempt to solve the extremely delicate problem before us, and that mistakes are much more easily corrected when the field of experiment is small than when it is large" (Maxwell, 1899, p. 132).

Thus, several classes modeled after Farrell's design were established in Manhattan at Public Schools 40, 77, 113, 111, and 180, and all were studied closely. By 1903 there were 10 such classes in both Manhattan and the Bronx, and the number of classes looked to further increase. The rationale used by the Board for establishing such a program districtwide was largely monetary. Farrell noted that

> ten percent of the school budgets of this country are spent in re-teaching children that which they have once been taught but have failed to learn. The educational budget for this country is four hundred millions of dollars. Forty millions of it is spent each year in re-teaching retarded children. (Farrell, 1923, p. 104)

Further, numerous children were dropping out of school without learning a trade, and it was believed that the majority of these students would become either criminals or victims of crime. With the goal of preventing a large population of unskilled labor from turning into a criminal class, it was necessary to sustain children's interest in school. Maxwell summed up the objective clearly: "The best of all ways to abolish truancy is to make schools so attractive that children will not willingly be absent" (Maxwell, 1902, p. 91).

Therefore, the impetus for classes such as Farrell's wasn't entirely altruistic. With exceptional children present in the already large classes, many felt that not only did the atypical child degenerate, but that the class was hindered as well, and the teacher's work was made harder and less effective. A 1918 New York Times article ("Backward Child") summarized the thoughts of the time:

> Besides getting nothing in the way of educational training themselves, these children have served as a drawback to the work of the rest of the class. It is an unfortunate phase of almost every school system that the class goes ahead only as fast as the slowest.

Even Farrell's mentor Lillian Wald, noted that "the settlement gladly helped her develop her theory of separate classes and special instruction for the defectives, not alone for their sakes, but to relieve the normal classes which their presence retarded" (Wald, 1915, p. 117).

As the unofficial expert regarding the special classes, Farrell continued to seek additional information so as to allow her to further refine her practice. To that end, she requested a leave of absence for the month of June 1903 "to investigate special teaching of backward and deficient children abroad" (Maxwell to Mack, May 12, 1903).

Study Abroad

In 1891 the School Board of London, England, had adopted a resolution establishing schools for children "who, by reason of physical or mental defect, cannot be properly taught in the ordinary standards or by ordinary methods, be established" (Maxwell, 1899, p. 130). In 1899, the National Board of Education investigated the special school program, the result of which was an amendment to the Elementary School Law of 1870 which provided national recognition and help for certified schools for such children. By 1903, the year Farrell traveled there, people in England had 10 years of experience working with these special classes and schools.

The idea of a completely separate educational program proved unsettling for Farrell, however, and the experience made her question "what particular kind of child could be educated only in a special class".

About 1% of the children attending schools in England at the time were considered to be physically or mentally defective, and the process of identifying and assigning children to special classes and schools was extremely methodical. Teachers, working under the supervision of a superintendent of special schools, first inspected all school children to determine if any appeared to suffer from physical or mental defects. The findings were then reported to the Superintendent of the Instruction of Physically and Mentally Defective Children who, along with a medical officer, examined the child. If the report was found to be correct, the child was sent to one of the centers for the instruction of defective children. In completely separate programs with separate facilities, doctors regularly examined these children, and extensive records were kept.

The idea of a completely separate educational program proved unsettling for Farrell, however, and the experience made her question "what particular kind of child could be educated only in a special class" (Farrell, 1903, p. 244).

Aware that in the initial stages, the London public had been opposed to offering these kinds of educational programs, she noted that "it is the boast of Americans that every child has the opportunity of school education but it is true that many children—through no fault of their own—get nothing from education. Not education but the right education should be our boast" (Farrell, 1903, p. 244).

Her experiences in Great Britain became the foundation for many of Elizabeth Farrell's future decisions regarding the ungraded classes. In fact, her decision to turn away from the concept of special schools and instead embrace the notion of classes within the public schools may have been cemented by what she observed in England. Capitalizing on the insight gained from her study of England's system, Farrell would continue her work in the ungraded class at the Henry Street School, further refining her ideas and putting them into practice in her own classroom. As a result, her name would become synonymous with this type of special instruction.

CHAPTER 2
An Evolving Practice

In his 1905 *Seventh Annual Report to the Board of Education,* Superintendent William H. Maxwell declared that the time of experiment is now ended—the ungraded classes have fully justified their existence—and for the future there remains ... the wide extension of this system" (p. 113). The Board of Education, with Superintendent Maxwell as its driving force, officially sanctioned the ungraded class program on February 14, 1906, and appointed Elizabeth Farrell Inspector of the Ungraded Class Department. With that designation, New York City became the first American city where this type of program was one person's sole responsibility. Reporting directly to the Board of Superintendents, Farrell had an extensive list of duties, including supervising the existing ungraded classes, aiding in the formation of new classes, cooperating in the examinations of children proposed for admittance to or removal from ungraded classes, assigning pupils, training teachers for these classes, and recommending teachers for leaves of absence to study approaches to serving this population of individuals.

To provide both Farrell and school principals a framework from which to operate, Maxwell issued several instructions regarding the special classes. Maxwell left the exact subject matter largely up to the school principals, but stressed that the students be taught practical skills (for girls, sewing and cooking; for boys, woodworking and use of tools). Further, Maxwell encouraged principals to obtain qualified individuals to lead these unique classes:

> The teacher who is to take up this work should be peculiarly adapted to it by nature. She should have insight into child nature, affection for children, and ability for leadership. She should be resourceful and inventive, reaching and quickening the spirit

of those who suffer. She should be wise and tactful, not only with children but with adults, for if she is to succeed, she must become the friend and adviser of the family, in order to get the co-operation so necessary to the best work of the child. She must be sanguine, cheerful, optimistic, patient, and have infinite capacity for taking pains. (Maxwell, 1906, p. 112)

This framework aside, Farrell's new position forced her to make many immediate decisions about the structure and future role of the ungraded class, not the least of which was determining whether or not to follow England's lead in creating completely separate classes in separate schools. Noting that the focus of this type of segregation of students was to prevent "the association in school of the mentally defective and the so-called normal child" (Farrell, 1911–1912, p. 13), Farrell chose to continue establishing special classes within existing schools, concluding that

The special school with its "separateness" emphasized in its construction, in its administration, differentiates, sets aside, classifies, and of necessity stigmatizes the pupils whom it receives. How could it be otherwise? Mental subnormality is so often associated with lack of beauty, proportion, and grace in the physical body of the child, the way we say mental subnormality and physical anomalies go hand-in-hand. Now bring together a rather large group—a hundred such children—and there assembled countless degrees of awkwardness and of slovenliness; infinite variations in overdevelopment or in arrested development and a dozen other mute witnesses of a mind infantile or warped. It would be next to impossible to save these helpless ones from the jibes of a not too kind world. The school which is to serve best must conserve the moral as well as the mental, the spiritual as well as the physical nature of the pupil. ("Elizabeth Farrell," 1935, p. 74)

In fact, Farrell wanted pupils in the the ungraded class to have the best of both worlds: "the opportunity for individual instruction while it presents to him, when he is able to grasp it, the chance of doing class work" (Farrell, 1911–1912, p. 15). To make her intentions in this regard clear, Farrell provided an illustration of how such an arrangement would work:

A child, hopelessly unable to comprehend even the simplest truths of arithmetic and further handicapped by a speech defect, which prohibited his taking part in a recitation period requiring spoken language, was found to have more than ordinary ability and interest in reading. The ungraded teacher was able to help him along the line of his interests. When he was able to write his answers he could attend a sixth-year class for those studies in which he could excel. His own self-respect and the increased prestige of the ungraded class were the result of his excellent work. In many schools the upper grade children are invited to visit the ungraded classroom to see the manual training exhibit. The children who were in danger of being pseudo-intellectual snobs because of scholastic achievements, realized when viewing the excellence of work identical with their own shopwork exercises, that to each has been given a talent, and that this group of "different" children have contributions to make to the life of the school no less valuable because they are unlike. (Farrell, 1911–1912, p. 15)

Referral, Assessment, and Placement

With the ungraded class program now an official part of the educational system in the City of New York, Farrell faced an increasing number of children being referred for special class placement, and she struggled to determine exactly which children might benefit from this kind of individualized instruction. Referrals came from a variety of sources: teachers and principals, physicians, the Bureau of Attendance, the Department of Physical Training, the Red Cross, and Children's Court, as well as the city's Department of Health. Those recommended for inclusion suffered from a wide variety of behavioral, academic, physical, or psychological problems and included nervous children who cried easily, were easily frightened, constantly moved, or had unusual anxieties; students with epilepsy; children who did not play or played with children much younger than themselves; over-conscientious children who exhibited irritability or a marked change in disposition; children with gross conduct disorders, including the truant, the incorrigible, and those who had "tantrums"; morally defective children who exhibited criminal tendencies; and those children whose progress in school was considered unsatisfactory or delayed.

Further compounding the problem, in 1903 an additional component of the Compulsory Education Provision was passed, requiring all children to attend school until 14 years of age (and through age 16 if they were not employed). Those in violation could be sent to truant/probationary schools for up to 2 years or until age 16, and their parents could be fined for failure to keep them in school. Although this law was not consistently enforced, it served to further increase the number of students referred to Farrell's program.

Originally concerned with children who didn't seem to "fit," irrespective of the cause, Farrell and the Board of Education began to focus more and more on children whose intelligence test scores suggested they could not benefit from typical class instruction. By 1905, Farrell and others calculated that perhaps as many as 12,000 children in New York City would be eligible for ungraded classes, by virtue of their being "exceptional to such a degree as to be unable" to participate in typical classes (Brown, 1905, p. 426).

Foreshadowing the kinds of self-contained special education classes offered decades later, Farrell refined the format of the ungraded classes even further, designing different classes to more appropriately meet the needs of the students:

> Ungraded classes differ in type. They are organized on the basis of chronological age as well as of mental age. There are classes for older high grade girls, classes for younger children, and so on. It is possible to differentiate ungraded classes on the principle of the children's most insistent need—classes for neurotic children, classes for psychopathic children, trade extension classes for girls. (Farrell, 1927, p. 6)

The initial method for selecting which children qualified for placement in the ungraded class program was established by the Board of Education. Principals reported to Farrell any child who—in the opinion of the teacher, Department of Health, or Department of Physical Training—was unable to do regular class work due to mental deficiency or any child 3 or more years behind in school. The teacher then completed a card with information based on observations of the student as well as any possible circumstances that might influence the child's condition: the economic condition of the family; home life; kindergarten attendance; number of terms in grade; school history and attendance; general knowledge; powers of attention and memory; motor skills; and habits of anger, obstinacy, cruelty, and truthfulness. This assessment was submitted to Farrell's office, for follow-up examination and assessment.

The examinations conducted by Farrell and the physician assigned to her department, when combined with the teacher's report, often yielded information that was useful to the teacher although the student might not be suited for the ungraded class. Farrell provided an example of such a case in her 1907 Annual Report to the Board of Education:

> An undersized, nervous, elf-like girl of nine years, she could keep awake and alert, except when required to sit at her desk. The moment she was still, her head was down and school forgotten; sleep would overpower her. Here was, indeed, a strange condition—a child apparently well, sleeping early in the school day. A word or two brought out the fact that this child, a mere baby, was required to rise at five o'clock in the morning, to sew buttons on boys' trousers until school time; after school in the afternoon, she was again compelled to take up the burden and work far into the night.
>
> This child knew that two different sizes of buttons were used, knew where to put them; she knew that ten buttons were put on one pair of trousers and twenty on two, but beyond that she could not go. This child was not a case for the ungraded class. The child had ability but it was used up each day before school received her. The fact of sleeping, in this particular case, was due to fatigue. Nature was doing her work; school had to wait. The fact, however, that this peculiarity was noted saved the child. It was found upon investigation that the father was saving his earnings, while his wife and this child were providing food and shelter for him and one younger child. (p. 622)

Although this referral process provided a "clear, comprehensive idea of the child, and his proper place" (Farrell, 1907, p. 622), Farrell ultimately viewed it as unsatisfactory as it left the selection of children to opinion and chance. By relying on this method, undue numbers of children with conduct disorders were referred to the program, although there was a complete absence of referrals for quiet, unobtrusive children, whom Farrell felt were often overlooked. Further, some school principals failed to refer students at all. In 1908, the second year of Farrell's department, only 116 of 180 Manhattan schools reported, only 12 of 42 in the Bronx reported, and only 74 of 148 Brooklyn schools reported any students for potential placement to Farrell's department (Farrell, 1908a, p. 602). To Farrell this represented a serious administrative problem. She longed for a more consistent manner of identifying and placing students in the ungraded classes, believing a satisfactory method must be based on the elimination of chance, opinion, and emotional factors.

As Inspector of the Department of Ungraded Classes, Farrell worked to create a referral procedure that would both meet her criteria and correctly place children in the special classes. Originally examining children referred for the ungraded classes once a week in Manhattan and Brooklyn at "clinic days," Farrell fought yearly for additional monies to fund more supervisory and medical staff positions. After the Board of Education approved Farrell's request in 1913, she started refining responsibilities and procedure to make testing and placement decisions more objective, establishing the Psycho-Educational Clinic. Part of the Department of Ungraded Classes, the clinic's function was to "reveal any underlying factors in the maladjustment of school children" (O'Shea, 1926, p. 310). The Psycho-Educational Clinic employed personnel from four different fields—psychology, social services, medicine, and education—all of whom worked together to determine which children were best served with placement in the ungraded department and which children could be best served through other means.

Farrell later noted that this more scientific approach had "inaugurated a new method of selecting children for special education".

The clinic psychologists administered intelligence tests and compared the results to reports from teachers. They administered norm-referenced performance, language, reading, and mathematics exams to students who scored below a certain intelligence score or otherwise had failed to make satisfactory progress. Farrell later noted that this more scientific approach had "inaugurated a new method of selecting children for special education" (Farrell, 1918–1920, p. 24).

The medical inspectors were responsible for examining all children proposed for placement in the ungraded classes. Working to determine the basis of any nervous or mental disorder, they often recommended the first line of treatment. They also looked for evidence of contagious diseases— ringworm, impetigo, scarlet fever, scabies, diphtheria, measles, chicken pox, pertussis, mumps, or tuberculosis—and sought to identify any issues that might impede a student's progress in school. This was intended to differentiate students who needed specialized instruction from those who could participate in a typical class if their physical challenges were addressed. Medical inspectors also had the responsibility of periodically re-examining all ungraded children "to ascertain the progress of the child and to furnish data for recommendations for discharge, exclusion, or promotion" (Farrell, 1921, p. 79). Removal from the ungraded classes could be made for three reasons: on the recommendation of the school principal that the child was ready to do grade-level work, when the child was 16 years old and no longer required to attend school, or if it was determined that the child required institutional care (Farrell, 1921, p. 12).

Visiting teachers employed in the Psycho-Educational Clinic fulfilled a social worker function. Initially volunteers, they performed a variety of services for the clinic: analyzing home conditions, securing information from interviews regarding the child's early life, obtaining parental cooperation, discussing problems with teachers and principals, assisting ungraded teachers, and summarizing and following up on clinic recommendations. In addition, they worked closely with social service agencies to get families registered and help them get financial help and medical care.

Despite the important function visiting teachers performed, there were very few employed in the clinic. In 1913–1914, the Psycho-Educational Clinic had only two visiting teachers serving approximately 3,000 children (Farrell, 1921, p. 94). Six years later, the number of children needing assistance had risen to approximately 6,000, yet there were still only three visiting teachers attached to the clinic (Farrell, 1921, p. 94). Despite Farrell's repeated requests, the Board of Education made few provisions for additional visiting teachers. As a result, the existing visiting teachers could handle only the most urgent of cases, and principals and teachers often hesitated to involve them until problems became severe.

The results of all of the Psycho-Educational Clinic examinations guided decisions about which manner of treatment and placement was most appropriate for individual students. Not all students reported were eligible for placement in the special classes; only about one of every three children referred was admitted to the ungraded classes. Others were recommended for continued inclusion in their typical class; the clinic offered suggestions regarding food and physical welfare, and these students' progress was monitored. Some children were sent to special classes for those with physical disabilities or to truant/probationary schools. And still other children were referred for institutionalization.

Not every parent whose child was referred and qualified for the ungraded classes was grateful for the intervention, however. At least one parent, Samuel Kastenburg of the Bronx, appealed to the magistrate in an effort to have his 11-year-old daughter removed from her ungraded class and returned to her original class. The magistrate, however, supported Farrell in her placement decision, saying that she had "supervision over ungraded classes and was qualified to decide" which students should be placed in the ungraded classes ("Court Upholds Act," 1922, p. 117).

Controversy, Debate, and Compromise

Although some viewed Farrell's Department of Ungraded Classes as a success, others—especially those on the Board of Estimates and Apportionment, the city department responsible for budgetary and financial concerns—viewed her expanding program with ever-increasing disdain. Considering the program an outgrowth of Superintendent Maxwell's drive to expand the school system's social agenda, the members of the Board of Estimates looked for ways to rein in the growing school budget and its "fads and frills" ("Superintendent Maxwell," 1906, p. 20). Superintendent Maxwell countered that

> No longer can it be maintained that education at the public expense is to be directed solely to secure "the survival of the fittest" or even of the fit. One of the prime checks of public education is to develop each child, fit or unfit, to his highest capacity, as far as conditions will permit, for the work and enjoyment of life. Education cannot perform miracles, but it can lighten the burdens of the defective by engendering habits that make for right living, and by training the capacity, no matter how slight it may naturally be, for work. (Maxwell, 1910, p. 103)

Farrell, greatly influenced by her Settlement colleagues, agreed with Maxwell that schools had a responsibility to assist children in reaching their potential:

> The function of the school is to provide an environment in which the abilities and capacities of each individual may unfold and develop in a manner that will secure his maximum social

efficiency. To secure this right environment, we must know the strength and the weakness of the individual's native endowment and we must know its modifications due to his experience. With these facts determined, the school life of the child will be tempered. The environment which society created for the education of the young will be so organized as to … insure to all the children the opportunity to succeed, to control and to accomplish. (Farrell, 1924, p. 103)

In 1912, after a decade-long battle of wills, the Board of Estimates and Apportionment asked Henry Herbert Goddard, the Director of Psychological Research at the Vineland Training School for Feeble-Minded Boys and Girls, to evaluate Farrell's program of ungraded classes. Although Goddard's primary charge at Vineland was to conduct research that might lead to identifying the causes of feeble-mindedness, he was intensely interested in the use of intelligence testing in schools. In 1910 Goddard had arranged for the Binet-Simon Intelligence Test to be translated for use in the United States and wanted to experiment with it on a large population of school children.

Although Goddard's report was highly critical of the ungraded class program, this was not for the reasons the Board of Estimates had anticipated.

Based on Goddard's perceived expertise in the education of the feeble-minded and the use of intelligence tests, the members of Board of Estimates anticipated a scathing rebuke of Maxwell's and Farrell's attempts to provide for those with low mentality. The results contained in Goddard's report, however, surprised them. Although Goddard's report was highly critical of the ungraded class program, this was not for the reasons the Board of Estimates had anticipated. Noting a steady increase in the number of ungraded classes, from 14 in 1906 to 131 in 1911–1912, with approximately 2,500 students enrolled, Goddard came to the conclusion that there were probably thousands of feeble-minded children teachers had failed to recognize and that New York should be providing for at least 15,000 students in the ungraded program. Rather than suggesting an abolishment of the program as the Board of Estimates had hoped, he instead encouraged its expansion.

Goddard reported that the system of placing children in the special classes was plagued by misdiagnosis, and that the program itself needed more supervisors and better-trained, skilled teachers—something Farrell had been saying for several years. Goddard went a step further, however, stating that the special class teachers were "painfully aware of their own lack of training and their own ability to do for the child what they feel must be done" (Goddard, 1912, pp. 361–381, as cited in Safford & Safford, 1996, pp. 181–184). Disagreeing with those who believed that "salvation lies in the ability to read books, to write letters, and to count millions," Goddard reported that a new curriculum was needed (Zenderland, 1998, p. 110). He recommended that the special classes surrender their attempts to teach academic content and instead follow the institutions' lead, with a curriculum focused on manual training, arguing that this would make life more pleasant for this population. At the heart of Goddard's report was the premise that the institution ought to be the laboratory for special classes.

The report sparked both controversy and protest. Superintendent Maxwell, feeling provoked by the Board of Estimates and wanting to rebut, faulted Goddard's logic in reaching the conclusion that the ungraded class program should be providing services to so many more children. Farrell, similarly, was outraged, and she attacked Goddard's survey results, criticizing Goddard for faulty research methods and questioning his sampling: She noted that he had visited only seven out of a possible 496 elementary schools and only one out of 21 possible high schools, with all of the schools located in either the Upper West Side, Lower East Side, Flushing, or the borough of Brooklyn.

Farrell also challenged Goddard's belief about the relationship between the institution and the special classes. Whereas Goddard stressed the similarities between the ungraded classes and the institutions, she saw her role as "emphasizing the points of resemblance and minimizing the differences between the regular grade child and the ungraded class child" (Farrell, 1913–1914, p. 75), articulating an early vision of an argument which would reemerge decades later in the debates over mainstreaming and inclusion. She believed the goal of the special classes was to return students back to their typical classes, and, therefore, the curriculum must not only teach academic content but also address diverse abilities and needs.

She further attacked Goddard's report, which used intelligence tests as the only diagnostic tool, stating that such tests alone would "not properly classify children for definite treatment or for detailed care and they are not infallible" (Farrell, 1913–1914, p. 68). Characterizing Goddard as a "research student in psychology," Farrell concluded that his report "lacks perspective," and was "concerned with conditions found at a given time, but lays no stress on the circumstances which brought them about nor on those in process of correcting them" (Farrell, 1913–1914, pp. 77–79). She noted that "to be unable to see the forest for the trees is sad. To have missed the vision is sadder still" (Safford & Safford, 1996, p. 183).

Farrell's sharp reply surprised Goddard. She had presented him with his first serious opposition, effectively countering his conceptualization of the relationship between institutions and the public school, and challenging his claims of expertise. By 1913, Goddard's report and Farrell's reply had reached the Board of Estimates, which appointed separate committees to review both reports and submit recommendations. In 1914, the committee reviewing Goddard's report suggested a compromise, endorsing some of Goddard's conclusions and some of Farrell's. The committee agreed with Goddard's recommendations for increased salary bonuses for ungraded class teachers, leave time for additional training, and more program personnel. It rejected, however, Goddard's statements regarding the number of children the New York School System should expect to serve, choosing instead to endorse Farrell's argument that such a number was unproven. The committee further rebutted Goddard's claims regarding curriculum. Most important, however, the committee chose not to endorse Goddard's beliefs regarding intelligence testing, refusing to adopt it as the main determination for placement in the ungraded classes.

Farrell's outrage over the reliance upon intelligence testing could do little to stem the tide, however. Despite the Board of Education's refusal to officially endorse intelligence testing, the use of intelligence tests by Goddard in the New York City Schools further served to legitimize them. In addition, Goddard had a captive audience in the teachers who attended Vineland's summer teacher education programs. By 1914 the movement had gained a foothold in schools, introduced not by the Board of Education but by teachers who were Vineland Training School graduates.

Intelligence and Ethnicity

In the first decade of the 20th century, Goddard was also collecting intelligence test data on immigrants entering the United States through Ellis Island. Based on this work, Goddard concluded that most immigrants entering the United States were of low intelligence. He rejected the idea that the tests might be biased or that there might be physical or psychological factors influencing the results, maintaining that intelligence testing "worked equally well with any child ... it was, therefore, unnecessary to analyze any other variables" (Zenderland, 1998, p. 265).

Goddard's position was reinforced by the release of *Laggards in Our Schools: A Study of Retardation and Elimination in City School Systems* (Ayres, 1909). Gullick and Ayres (1908) had reviewed data from 15 schools in New York City, including 20,000 students in Manhattan alone, and concluded that boys exhibited a higher percentage of retardation than did girls, that the smallest percentage of retardation was found in Germans, and the highest percentage of retardation was found in Italians.

Disregarding her own immigrant background, she had earlier concurred that "marked abilities, as well as marked disabilities, may be explained only by referring to ancestry and home".

The federal government, through the Ellis Island immigration authority, sought to prohibit the feeble-minded from entering the country by requiring intelligence tests of those suspected of being of low mentality. Reports of Goddard's research contributed to the passage of the Immigration Restriction Act of 1924 and the increased deportation of immigrants for reasons of mental deficiency. The Act, which remained in effect until 1965, placed the heaviest restrictions on eastern and southern Europeans—Italians, Ashkenazi Jews, Russians, and Hungarians—national groups Goddard, in his research, had found to be feeble-minded.

Farrell followed this developing debate closely. With more and more immigrant children being referred to the ungraded classes, she could not completely ignore research that suggested a correlation between ethnic origin and intelligence. Disregarding her own immigrant background, she had earlier concurred that "marked abilities, as well as marked disabilities, may be explained only by referring to ancestry and home" (Farrell, 1907, p. 621).

It appears, however, that Farrell may have had conflicting feelings about the weight given solely to nationality, as she made contradictory statements regarding the correlation between heredity and intelligence. In her 1909 report to the Board of Education, she cautioned that the apparent increase in "insanity among the immigrant population" (p. 644) may have been due to extenuating circumstances: The identification of children who were abnormally slow was more likely to be made in schools in which there were large numbers of foreign-born children or children of foreign-born parents. She concluded that "schools in such neighborhoods are crowded as a rule and the exceptional child must be removed from the regular class in order to make conditions bearable at all" (p. 644).

The next year, however, Farrell appeared to reverse course again. In her 1910-1911 report to the Board of Education, she quoted A. F. Tredgold, an English neurologist and author, who believed that the causes of mental deficiency fell into two categories: "morbid heredity, where some ancestral, pathological condition modifies the parental germoplasm before conception of the child," and "adverse environment, where some external factor (disease or injury) affects the embryo in the uterus, the babe at birth or the growing child after birth" (p. 19). By noting Tredgold's belief that "90 per cent of all cases of mental deficiency are due to morbid heredity" (p. 19), Farrell seems to have agreed that heredity was the larger issue of concern.

Still, it appears Farrell vacillated between accepting the "science" that correlated the two variables and rejecting the arguments wholeheartedly. One can assume a variety of circumstances were at play in Farrell's personal and professional lives which may have influenced her acknowledgment of such a correlation, including her own immigrant history, the Progressive philosophy of the Henry Street Settlement and its residents, and the research considered "best science" at the time, as well as her own observations of the population being placed in the ungraded classes.

Changes in Leadership

Throughout this embattled period, Superintendent Maxwell publicly supported Farrell's decisions as she fought to increase the size of the Department of Ungraded Classes and further clarify its mission. After taking repeated periods of leave for illness, however, Maxwell was forced to resign in 1917. The Board of Education, in deference to Maxwell's role in leading the school system for so many years, offered him the position of Superintendent Emeritus with a salary of $10,000 a year for life. Maxwell was succeeded by William Ettinger in 1918 and later by William O'Shea in 1924, under whose tenure Farrell served until her death in 1932.

Both Ettinger and O'Shea continued to provide the unwavering support that Farrell had experienced under Maxwell's leadership. With this continuing support, she would professionalize the role of the ungraded teacher.

CHAPTER 3
Shaping the Profession

In her role as Inspector of the Department of Ungraded Classes, Elizabeth Farrell faced many of the same issues that special education directors and administrators deal with today. Perhaps most critical among them was the shortage of qualified teachers to meet the demands of the number of ungraded classes required in the public schools throughout New York City. As head of the department it was considered one of Farrell's chief duties to find those teachers who had a natural aptitude for working in the ungraded classroom.

It was no easy task. Every year the number of ungraded classes throughout the school district grew. In 1906, when Farrell became Inspector of the Ungraded Department, there were only 14 classes; 15 years later there were over 250 (Farrell, 1921, p. 78). To assist Farrell in identifying additional ungraded teachers, the Board of Examiners began to conduct competitive examinations. These exams were open to women with at least 3 years teaching experience, as well as teachers in private schools and school districts outside of New York City. The examination consisted of three parts: written, oral, and practical. The written portion included two papers, one on the methods of ungraded instruction and the other on principles of education. The practical exam consisted of skill demonstration in such areas as basketry, piano playing, drawing, and sewing. The oral exam was a practicum of sorts, where the candidate was put in charge of an ungraded class in order to observe her use of the English language and her classroom management ability. If the applicant did not hold a regular license to teach in the New York City public school system, a certificate of physical fitness, along with proof of vaccinations and citizenship was required.

For the most part, however, Farrell was forced to resort to less than ideal methods to secure teachers for ungraded classes. One of these was to ask for volunteers among the already licensed teachers employed within the school system. Occasionally, a teacher would volunteer because of a real interest in helping struggling children. Often, though, teachers would volunteer because those employed in the special classes made between $1,900 and $3,250 per year, a larger salary than other classroom teachers. Farrell was in favor of increased salary amounts for ungraded class teachers, believing they rendered a valuable service and that the salaries were not commensurate with their difficult work. She felt that substantial increases might induce larger numbers of teachers to prepare themselves for a career in the ungraded classes.

Farrell was in favor of increased salary amounts for ungraded class teachers, believing they rendered a valuable service and that the salaries were not commensurate with their difficult work.

Compounding the difficulty that Farrell faced in recruiting teachers was the problem of training, and there were few programs in the area able to provide adequate instruction in the methods of teaching this cohort of children. The summer course sponsored by the Vineland Training School for Feeble-Minded Girls and Boys was based on a philosophy that was distinctly different from Farrell's; Vineland's superintendent advocated "education in special classes until sexual maturity, to be followed by locally funded municipal custodial industrial institutions in the cities and by rural colonies to reclaim waste land" (Doll, 1988, p. 7). Another program, offered during the school year through Teachers College at Columbia University, was perhaps one of the best known and more in sync with Farrell's programming ideas (she served as an instructor there)—but it required teachers to travel miles after the school day had ended. Farrell noted that

> One teacher who took up ungraded work spent $150 and for five years has taken three hours a week in one of the local colleges. To take only the specialized work on the subject which was offered in the city necessitated miles of travel after the school day was over. This outlay of money and strength many good teachers are unable to make. (Farrell, 1910–1911, pp. 26–27)

PHOTOS & ARCHIVE MATERIALS

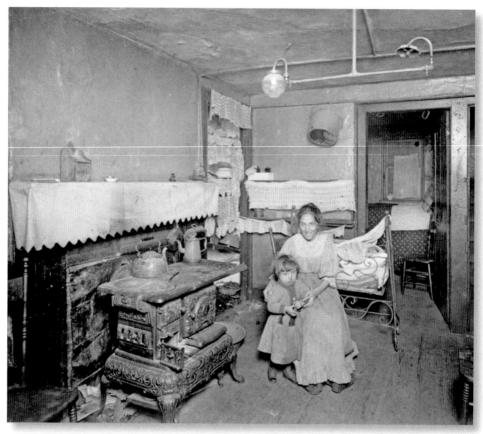

Tenement room in Manhattan's Lower East Side.

Progressive Reformer Lillian Wald.

Henry Street Settlement nurse on assignment in the Lower East Side.

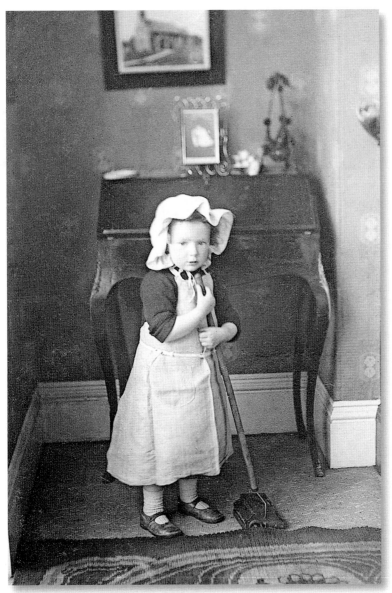

The 1899 Compulsory Education Provision meant that children who earlier had spent their time working or on the streets would now be required to attend school. Many schools were not equipped to handle the new deluge of students.

If it was determined that a child was prevented from learning due to a physical defect, and it was possible to treat the defect, then it was treated while the child remained in the grade so that he or she could return to normal work.

Grade school class, early 1900s.

"One of the prime checks of public education is to develop each child, fit or unfit, to his highest capacity, as far as conditions will permit, for the work and enjoyment of life." (Maxwell, 1910, p. 103)

Elizabeth Farrell and her first Ungraded class.

New Jersey's Vineland Training School. Henry Herbert Goddard had a captive audience in the teachers who were in attendance at the summer teacher education programs sponsored by the school. The intelligence testing movement was not introduced by the Board of Education, but by teachers who were Vineland Training School graduates.

Goddard went on to gather intelligence test data on immigrants entering the United States through Ellis Island. Based on this work, Goddard further concluded that most immigrants entering the United States were of low intelligence.

Elizabeth E. Farrell.

Elizabeth Farrell faced many of the same issues that special education administrators deal with today. Perhaps most critical among them was the shortage of
qualified special education teachers.

Meeting at the George Washington University for the national Council for the
Education of Exceptional Children as part of the National Education Assocaition
convention.

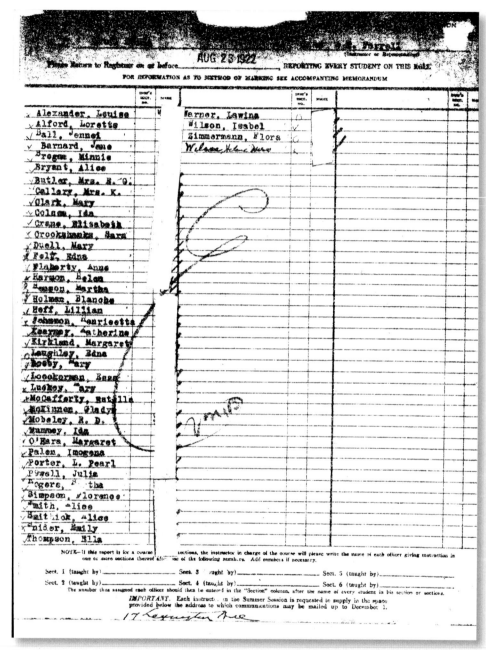

INST'S SECT. NO.	NAME	INST'S SECT. NO.	MARK		INST'S SECT. NO.
	Alexander, Louise		Werner, Lavina		
	Alford, Loretta		Wilson, Isabel		
	Ball, Jennei		Zimmermann, Flora		
	Barnard, Jane		Wilson, Helen Mary		
	Brogan, Minnie				
	Bryant, Alice				
	Butler, Mrs. R. Q.				
	Callary, Mrs. K.				
	Clark, Mary				
	Colnon, Ida				
	Crane, Elizabeth				
	Crookshanks, Sara				
	Duell, Mary				
	Felt, Edna				
	Flaherty, Anna				
	Harmon, Helen				
	Henson, Martha				
	Holman, Blanche				
	Hoff, Lillian				
	Johnson, Henrietta				
	Kearney, Catherine				
	Kirkland, Margaret				
	Laughley, Edna				
	Mosby, Mary				
	Loockerman, Essa				
	Luckey, Mary				
	McCafferty, Estella				
	McKinnon, Gladys				
	Mobeley, R. D.				
	Mumney, Ida				
	O'Hara, Margaret				
	Palen, Imogene				
	Porter, L. Pearl				
	Powell, Julia				
	Rogers, Bertha				
	Simpson, Florence				
	Smith, Alice				
	Smithick, Alice				
	Snider, Emily				
	Thompson, Ella				

NOTE—If this report is for a course / sections, the instructor in charge of the course will please write the name of each officer giving instruction in one or more sections thereof after one of the following numbers. Add numbers if necessary.

Sect. 1 (taught by) _____ Sect. 3 (taught by) _____ Sect. 5 (taught by) _____
Sect. 2 (taught by) _____ Sect. 4 (taught by) _____ Sect. 6 (taught by) _____

The number thus assigned each officer should then be entered in the "Section" column, after the name of every student in his section or sections.

IMPORTANT. Each instructor in the Summer Session is requested to supply in the space provided below the address to which communications may be mailed up to December 1.

17 Lexington Ave

Class roster for course taught by Elizabeth Farrell at Columbia University, signed with her initial. Founders of the International Council for Exceptional Children (established 1922) included students from this class.

Minutes of the Organization of the
Council for the Education of
Exceptional Children.

On August 10, 1922, a group of people interested in
Education for all types of Special Children met together
at a dinner conference in New York City for the purpose of
organizing an association of Special Class education.

The business meeting was opened by Miss Elizabeth E.
Farrell, Inspector of Ungraded Classes, N. Y. C , who acted
as chairman.

The first order of business was the election of officers.

Miss Alice C Smithick, conductor of Psychological Tests,
Montclair, New Jersey, nominated Miss Farrell for president.
The nominations were moved to be closed, seconded and carried
and Miss Farrell was unanimously elected President.

Miss La Vinia Warner, Director of Special Education, Ohio
University, Athens, Ohio, was nominated secretary by Miss Hen-
rietta A. Johnson, Supervisor of Special Education, Oakland,
California. The nominations were closed, seconded and carried.

Miss Jessie B. Dori g, Assistant Supervisor of Ungraded
classes, N. Y. C. was elected Vice-President and Miss Estella
McCafferty, Principal of Jackson Opportunity School, Kansas
City, was elected treasurer.

The President then asked for suggestions for a name for
the new organization. Several names were given and discussed.
The name of International Council for the Education of Exceptional Children, was proposed by Miss Jennie L. Hall, Superintendent of Girl's Vocational School, Aligarh, India. It
was moved by Miss Smithick that this name be adopted. The
motion was carried.

It was voted that the International Council for the Education of Exceptional Children hold its First Annual Meeting
in February, 1923, at the same time and place that the Dept, of
Superintendence of the National Educational Association holds
its meeting.

The question of membership was then announced by the
President. It was moved that the membership include any person
who is interested in the Education of Exceptional Children.

The next order of business was that of membership fees.
It was moved by Miss Imogene Palem, Teacher of Lip Reading,
Toronto, Canada that the fee for one year be $1.00. The motion
was carried.

A motion was then made by Miss Johnson that there be one
grade of membership, active. The motion was carried.

Minutes of the organizational meeting of the International Council for Exceptional
Children, August 1922.

On August 10, 1922 eighteen students at Teachers College in the summer
session, decided that the next step in special education was fellowship,
that they ought to get together, and know what the other is doing.
    In that group were people from India, people from Sweden and one
person from South Africa. That is why the Council was called international.
It is truly international in its fellowship, in its membership.
....

    Those who we5ebher last night and saw what the eighth annual dinner
could be must know, must appreciate that this baby, this International
Council, eight years old, is vigorous and strong: it is to be reckoned
with in educational programs in this country - and Superintendents or no
Superintendents, we are going to meet every year.

    One of the tendencies is that this good type of educational training
which we provide for our children is affecting all school systems. When
you hear of ability groupings, you can look back to a small group of people
who, before the term was in general use, were talking about the desirability
of teaching children what they could learn, developing their powers,
instead of emphasizing their deficiencies.
    We did that- the IC group did it - before any other school group
had ever dreamed of it ... That was the first tendency/ And we want to go
back, each one, to our schools and advocate that children must be taught
according to what they have and not according to what we think they ought
to have.

    another tendency - the development of differential curriculum all
over the country.
....

    In NY, I hope we are going to have industrial schools, schools of
inddustry taught by workmen with some knowledge of teaching processes; and
we are going to transfer into these district schools of industry the
adolescent boy and girl, who will learn there under the conditions of
industry, under the conditions of a work-day life, those trades and occup-
ations which will help them when they go into the larger fields of work.

....
    ICEC organized for two purposes: One, to develop teaching techniques
that are needed in the various types of special classes; and, two,
to develop curricula, units of subject matter, projects that can be
presented at meetings of this kind and can be taken home by those who attend,
put into use there and then reported back the next year as to the success
or failure of that particular unit of work.

....

    Now, my last work, The jails are full of your failures - all of you.
Your state didn't ask you to be a teacher. You came and offered yourself
as a teacher/ And I want to challenge the right of any person to be a tr.
of another unless that person will exhaust every resource to be a better
and a better teacher.   If these men in jail - and the women, too- had had

the kind of teachers that this government expected them to have, I question
whether the jails would be full. I am aware that there is subnormality,
psycho½athic conditions, poverty, and what not. But one of the greatest
reasons is the lack of right educational opportunity.

I want every teacher here to think now of her failures, of the men and the
women whose lives were cut short in their opportunity, because we were not
well-trained enough, because the science of education was not an instrument
in our hands. How many people are less than they should be because we lack
the artistry of creating interest, because we lack the artistry of making
attractive the knowledge of the world?

As we consecrate again, this moment, our lives to the education of this
country, let us say, with Wells, "It is a race between destruction and
education. I am a teacher, and destruction shall never win."

Elizabeth Farrell's closing comments at the eighth annual meeting of the
International Council for Exceptional Children, 1930.

Elizabeth E. Farrell

1870   1932
IN MEMORY OF
ELIZABETH FARRELL
PIONEER TEACHER
OF BACKWARD CHILDREN
IN NEW YORK CITY
SHE DEVOTED HER LIFE
TO THE DEVELOPMENT OF
THE UNGRADED CLASSES
AND LEFT TO ALL CHILDREN
IN NEED OF SPECIAL HELP
THE ASSURANCE THAT
THEY MIGHT FIND IT
IN THE PUBLIC SCHOOLS

Plaque at CEC Headquarters, Arlington, VA.

In 1906, the Board of Education attempted to address this thorny issue, authorizing 3 months' leave with full pay for ungraded teachers so that they could attend an appropriate program. Farrell, however, felt that although this was a good first step, it didn't alleviate the burden on ungraded teachers, their families, or the department. She proposed establishing a 3-month graduate course at the Brooklyn Training School for teachers assigned to ungraded classes (possibly so she could design it to specifically coordinate with New York City's ungraded class program).

Teacher Training and Professional Development

In 1912, Farrell's idea was adopted by the Board of Education. Fifteen teachers were selected to attend the Brooklyn Training School in cohort groups. The first group of ungraded teachers reported in November of that year, with the second group beginning the course of study the following April. Teachers selected for cohort groups came from two areas: the first group held a regular teaching license and had 3 years' successful teaching experience in typical classrooms. These teachers were assigned to teach in ungraded classes with the appropriate salary for 2 years, at the end of which they must have taken the exam and obtained an ungraded teaching license. The majority of the teachers enrolled in the Brooklyn Training School's graduate course were secured by this method. The second group of teachers was appointed from eligible lists as the result of ungraded teacher examinations. They had to be between 21 and 46 years old and meet all the academic, professional, and special qualifications required in the Board of Education by-laws.

The Brooklyn Training School curriculum was organized to provide key information on the education of children who were placed in ungraded classrooms, and it intended to promote development of those skills necessary to be an ungraded class teacher. In one report, Farrell described some of the courses:

Psychology: The course will aim to give a knowledge of the nature and the activity of mind from the standpoint of normal development.... Pathological conditions of attention, memory, will, etc. will be analyzed.

Physiology: Abnormalities and pathological conditions found in school children will be studied and their relation to normal mental development demonstrated.

Methods: Attention will be called to the necessity of establishing correct fundamental or primary habits—hence the obligation to present the concrete rather than the abstract, materials rather than symbols in the beginning work. (Farrell, 1913–1914, pp. 19–20)

During their course of study, the Brooklyn Training School teachers also worked in ungraded classrooms under the supervision of Farrell or one of her assistant inspectors. Ungraded class teachers were observed and evaluated, and observations were followed up with a conference during which both strong and weak teaching areas were identified and means of improvement discussed.

Eventually, the course of study at the Brooklyn Training School was extended to 3 years, and the curriculum was differentiated to identify those teachers who seemed best suited to teach the elementary, middle, or upper grades, classifying students according to their ability. Growth in the number of program applicants may have allowed the Board of Education to create more stringent requirements, yet the program proved such a success in securing qualified teachers that Farrell recommended that similar programs be established in other parts of the city.

As inspector of the department, Farrell sought ways to encourage professional growth among its members. Once employed, ungraded teachers were assigned to a small group for a 2-year period. These groups, which included experienced teachers, met monthly for what amounted to professional development. They gave demonstrations; formulated supply lists; participated in discussions; examined issues surrounding health education, practical applications for math, manual training, industrial, household, and fine arts; and learned about the practical and economical use of industrial supplies. Ungraded teachers also participated in periodic meetings with psychologists from agencies involved with ungraded classes in which they would discuss articles in professional periodicals and exchange views regarding psychological materials and evaluation procedures.

Farrell did not confine her work to fostering professional growth to her department, however. She spent numerous years working to educate students at the university level. In 1906, the year she was appointed inspector of the department, Farrell received a Bachelor of Science degree from New York University (NYU), and was later invited to work as a lecturer in its School of Pedagogy. Farrell taught four courses at NYU related to the supervision and instruction of special classes:

- Observation and Practice, where students had the opportunity to observe special classes and participate in readings, discussions, and lectures;
- Observation and Practice–Advanced Course, where students continued the observation work begun in the earlier course;
- Organization and Management of Special Classes, which covered the principles and practices of the special classes and discussed factors regarding growth, supervision, and classification; and
- Standards for Measuring Instruction, where a student taught a group of ungraded children and had her work observed and discussed.

Farrell also served as a lecturer at Teachers College, Columbia University, from 1915 until her death in 1932, co-teaching several classes with a colleague. Together, they taught and supervised advanced students in graduate courses who conducted investigations or experiments in the special classes. These graduate courses included Methods of Teaching in Special Classes, where Farrell reviewed the methods and subject matter of the elementary school class needed by these children as well as the diagnosis of failure; and Supervision of Special Classes, which was designed for students who planned on becoming principals, supervisors, instructors, or supervisory officers in teacher training schools.

Farrell also worked to improve the ungraded teaching profession through Ungraded *magazine, a professional periodical sponsored by the Ungraded Classroom Teachers Association.*

Farrell also worked to improve the ungraded teaching profession through *Ungraded* magazine, a professional periodical sponsored by the Ungraded Classroom Teachers Association. At its inception in May of 1915, Farrell participated as a member of the magazine's advisory board and later became even more involved, taking first the position of associate editor and later assuming the position of editor—as well as regularly contributing articles. She also used the magazine as a vehicle to publish research conducted in the ungraded classes, and her relationship with *Ungraded* and the Ungraded Classroom Teachers Association provided her with a platform to showcase her views regarding children with exceptionalities and their unique needs in the classroom.

Professional Associations

Farrell also wanted to promote collegial relationships and communication among those who worked with children with special educational needs. Seeking to recognize the looming impact that the field of applied psychology and intelligence testing would have on the placement of children in ungraded classes, she and several others who worked in education became members of the American Psychological Association (APA). As the number of these applied psychologists grew, they looked to the APA for leadership.

The APA and the New York State Psychological Association

At the time, the American Psychological Association was strongly committed to the scientific side of psychology. To meet what they believed to be a growing need, Farrell, her assistant, Elizabeth Walsh, and her colleague Leta Hollingworth of Teachers College attempted to organize the New York State Association of Consulting Psychologists at a meeting of the American Psychological Association in 1916. Unfortunately, due to a lack of interest on the part of the APA, the new organization didn't gain momentum. But years later the organization resurfaced under the leadership of psychologist David Mitchell, and the New York State Association of Consulting Psychologists (later the New York State Psychological Association) became the first state-level psychological association—as well as the first to advocate for the recognition of the profession of psychology. Organized for the purposes of promoting "high standards of professional qualifications for consulting psychologists" and to "stimulate research work in the field of psychological analysis and evaluation" ("Notes and News," 1921, p. 439), membership in the organization was limited to those who had a minimum of 2 years' graduate work in psychology. This new organization valued applied psychology at a time when the American Psychological Association's emphasis was on pure and applied research.

In 1922, the APA published a pamphlet by the American Red Cross entitled *Examination of Pre-School Age Children: Examination of Children Upon Registering Before Entering School*. The pamphlet, detailing intelligence test data on 1,113 children entering kindergarten and Grade 1A in eight New York City public schools, was created in cooperation with Farrell and the Department of Ungraded Classes. The goal of the publication was to provide data for principals to use in identifying children for the ungraded classes (McCarthy, 1956). The pamphlet also recommended a schedule for examining children in June, so that any physical issues could be addressed during the summer (through the coordination of services of the school nurses and the American Red Cross)—thereby eliminating the interruption of school attendance by first-year students. This schedule might also ease the burden on her Department of Ungraded Classes by reducing the number of children referred to the Psycho-Educational Clinic once the school year began.

The National Education Association

In 1897, upon petition of Alexander Graham Bell, the National Education Association (NEA)'s Department of Special Education was formed. In 1911 Farrell became vice-president of this division, and was later its president. It was in this leadership capacity that she promoted collegiality, bringing together individuals representing day and residential schools, clinics, private agencies, state departments of education, hospitals, and universities. The division disintegrated in 1918, however, due to a lack of publications, meager committee work, and limited funds (Wooden, 1962). After the dissolution of the NEA's Department of Special Education, an organization was needed which would fill the void and keep the teachers of these special classes in touch with each other and with developments in the field.

The Founding of the Council for Exceptional Children

In August 1922, Farrell was teaching courses at Teachers College. A group of 18 students enrolled in her courses asked her to attend a meeting to discuss ways to promote fellowship among educators as well as a means of exchanging ideas among workers in special education. The 11 attendees at that meeting established the International Council for the Education of Exceptional Children, unanimously electing Farrell president (see Appendix; Warner, "Minutes," 1922; Warner, 1942, p. 245).

At that first organizational meeting, the Council identified three aims:
- Emphasize the education of the "special child"—rather than his identification or classification.
- Establish professional standards for teachers in the field of special education.
- Unite those interested in the educational problems of the "special child." (Warner, n.d., p. 1).

Membership was open to any person who was interested in the education of children with exceptionalities, and dues were $1 per year.

At the first annual meeting of the International Council in 1923, Farrell spoke about the purpose of such a teaching organization and the responsibilities of those who were called to join:

> The International Council for the Education of Exceptional Children will be the clearinghouse of knowledge useful to teachers in their special fields. The Council will be for teachers the authoritative body on questions of subject matter, method and school or class organization. At its annual meeting it hopes to present ideas proved to be useful in the training of exceptional children. The Council hopes to stimulate the teaching of children at least to the extent that psychologists have stimulated classification on the basis of intellectual power. The Council will stand back of its membership in demanding high professional qualifications for those designated to serve in its fields. It will demand freedom for its members as practitioners. It will promote the idea that educational work, whether in institutions or in public day schools, must be in the hands of and directed by men and women trained in the science and art of education.... With modesty and great humility all its members accept responsibilities of their calling. They hope that because of their efforts public education in this country will be less machine-made and more individual; that the schools of this country will use the ability of each pupil group to its maximum; that the school will fit its burden to the back which bears it; that it will bring the opportunity of successful achievement to every child. (Kirk & Lord, 1974, pp. 16–21).

Even in its early years, the Council focused on teacher training, professional collegiality, and program and instructional design. In 1924, at the second annual meeting of the Council, a new section of the professional journal *Ungraded*, of which Farrell was editor, was designated to serve as the official pronouncement of the Council, thus linking together the journal, the Ungraded Classroom Teachers Association, and the Council.

At the fourth annual meeting in 1926, Farrell stepped down as president of the Council, taking instead the position of vice-president. By then there were over 400 members in the organization, representing 33 states, the

District of Columbia, Canada, India, and Holland—reflecting perhaps both the need for such an organization as well as Farrell's strength in fostering its growth. In 1929, at the Council's seventh annual meeting, Farrell was honored with a tribute and awarded lifetime membership.

The Legacy of Elizabeth Farrell

At its tenth annual meeting in 1932, the Council passed a resolution noting Farrell's silver anniversary with the Department of Ungraded Classes. There was also a party in her honor in March of that year, at the Hotel Astor in New York City. Farrell received congratulatory telegrams from numerous influential people familiar with her work, including Eleanor Roosevelt. A message from the United States Office of Education noted that she had "pioneered in this important field of education," in promoting "the right of the child to be dealt with intelligently as society's charge and not its outcast…. The whole system of education has been modified to consider improved conditions for all children ("Ungraded Classes," 1932, p. 13).

In her absence, Elizabeth A. Walsh, Farrell's assistant, was appointed acting inspector. Farrell passed away unexpectedly during treatment on October 15, 1932.

Not long after the celebration, Farrell requested a leave of absence from her position to travel to Battle Creek, Michigan, and the Cleveland Clinic, in Cleveland, Ohio, for treatment of a heart ailment. In her absence, Elizabeth A. Walsh, Farrell's assistant, was appointed acting inspector. Farrell passed away unexpectedly during treatment on October 15, 1932.

Her family accompanied her body back to Utica, New York, her hometown, to be buried in the family plot. An editorial in *The New York Times* acknowledged how important her work had been, in noting that "the moral of Miss Farrell's educational success is 'individualization'" ("Elizabeth Farrell," 1932, p. 5). The faculty of the Oswego Normal and Training School similarly paid tribute to her:

Her contributions will continue to function in the future work of all teachers of special classes and will, through the years, continue to make it possible for handicapped children to have the opportunity for more efficient living and greater happiness as well as converting possible social liabilities into assets.

She leaves us a legacy of work well done, of wisdom directed persistently toward the solution of the difficult problems in her chosen field, of loyalty to the profession and the noble ideals which it professes. We shall always cherish her memory as that of a wise and virtuous teacher. ("Memorial," 1932)

Farrell's passing was keenly felt by her New York City community and school system. A memorial service held in her honor in February of 1933 at the Cosmopolitan Club in New York included many of the same speakers as at the 25th anniversary celebration the previous year. Grace Ball, the president of the Council, sent a telegram to the event, noting that with her passing

The International Council for Exceptional Children has lost its founder, a wise counselor, a rare friend. For her clear vision, her unfailing help, her warm championship of children, especially these handicapped little ones under her care, she will ever be a living influence in those whose lives she touched. We mourn her passing; we rejoice in her living.

The faculty and students of Oswego Normal and Training School dedicated a bronze tablet to Farrell to recognize her contribution in establishing their Department of Special Training in 1916 and her influence on the field of education. Dr. John H. Finley wrote the inscription:

In memory of Elizabeth Farrell, Class of 1895, Oswego State Normal and Training School, who gave her life that the least might live as abundantly as their handicaps of mind or body permitted. A teacher of the atypical, the subnormal, the dull of spirit, the slow of speech, the inert. In teaching them she also gave instruction in the method by which the normal, the bright, and alert should be taught. Beginning with a little group of boys in the Lower East Side of Manhattan, she became the tutelary of the ungraded classes for all New York City, demanding no child too atypical to be neglected....Keep we the altars kindled. Guard we the sacred fires. ("Dedication," n.d.)

Epilogue

K imberly Kode's welcome update and expansion of *Elizabeth Farrell and the History of Special Education* is important for contemporary special educators, psychologists and diagnosticians, school administrators, and historians focused on the history of disability for a number of reasons. Reading this new edition, one is struck with how contemporary some of the ideas and issues that emerged in the opening decades of the 20th century feel 100 years later. Consider these quotes from the Introductory chapter; aren't they as relevant today as they were in the early 1900s?

> Farrell sought to adopt a similar methodological procedure of examination and record-keeping—but one that was not differentiated by separate programs, separate facilities, and separate schools, believing such a policy would stigmatize and isolate students with special education needs.

> Similarly, Farrell advocated for a well-rounded assessment of student's abilities, rather than a reliance on intelligence testing as the single measure for placement of a child in the ungraded class.

Farrell's progressive nature is best reflected, I think, in her entanglement with Henry Herbert Goddard, the psychologist and mental testing pioneer who introduced the Binet-Simon test to an American audience and proceeded to try to establish it as the means to classify and, essentially, segregate people who were then deemed to be "feebleminded." Goddard's story is fairly well known, and my colleague David Smith and I have written about it extensively in our book *Good Blood, Bad Blood: Science, Nature, and the Myth of the Kallikaks* (Smith & Wehmeyer, 2012). As *Elizabeth Farrell and the History of Special Education* effectively relates, Farrell took on Goddard and the "intelligence men" who were pushing mental testing as a means to identify—and, at that time, institutionalize—people who were increasingly being seen as menaces to society. I remember being amused by Elizabeth Farrell's tenacity in what were clearly long odds against her. That she basically was able to come to a draw with Goddard was, in essence, a success for efforts to educate students who were not succeeding in schools in the public education sphere, rather than the quickly growing institutional system. True, as was noted by Farrell's mentor and pioneering humanitarian Lillian Wald, some of the reasons that the special school system evolved was to "relieve the normal classes which their presence retarded," still, it seems overwhelmingly evident that Farrell acted out of an abundance of empathy and a commitment to social justice.

I mention "intelligence men" in the previous paragraph for a reason. That is, when one reads about the history of intelligence and intelligence testing in our country, what one reads about are men. I take the term *intelligence men* from Raymond Fancher's 1985 book, *The Intelligence Men: Makers of the IQ Controversy*. Each chapter in Fancher's book discusses one of these "makers of the IQ controversy," and they are all men: John Stuart Mill, Francis Galton, James McKeen Cattell, Alfred Binet, Charles Spearman, William Stern, Henry Herbert Goddard, Robert Mearns Yerkes, Lewis Madison Terman, David Wechsler, Cyril Lodowic Burt, Arthur Jensen, and Leon Kamin. One of the underlying themes in *Good Blood, Bad Blood* was the ever-present issue of gender discrimination and the lack of opportunities for women in the newly emerging fields of psychology and special education. One of the key figures in the Kallikak Family saga was a field worker named Elizabeth Kite, who was trained by Goddard at the Vineland Training School to go out among the families of some of the inmates of the Training School and collect data about their family background, medical history, and so forth (eventually used to justify Goddard's eugenic world view). When she went to work in this rather menial role, she was fresh from several years of study in England, France, Germany, and Switzerland. Kite earned a teaching certificate from the Sorbonne (in Paris), studied English history at the University of London, and took post-graduate courses in psychology at the University of Pennsylvania. She was fluent in French and translated, during her tenure at Vineland, the works of Alfred Binet (developer of the first intelligence test) for Goddard, and, after Vineland, the letters between George Washington and Pierre L'Enfant, the engineer who designed Washington, DC. She was later in life awarded an honorary doctorate from Villanova University and served as archivist of the American Catholic Historical Association. And yet, in 1910, the best position she could secure was as a field worker for the Vineland Training School.

Women are notably missing from the narratives that reflect the history (direct and indirect) of our field. Women like Dorothea Dix and Jane Addams and Lillian Wald are mentioned in reference to the establishment of asylums and settlements and other ways that, in their time, were more humanistic approaches to supporting the poor and other marginalized peoples. But, do a Google search for the pioneers of "humanistic psychology" and see if you can find a woman listed between Jung, Maslow, Rogers and George Kelly. There were, certainly, early pioneers in the fields of psychology, but about the only one who gets any recognition among the "intelligence men" is Leta Stetter Hollingsworth, Professor of Education at Teachers College, Columbia University, and pioneering author of *The Psychology of the Subnormal* (1920) and *The Psychology of the Adolescent* (1928), whose biography is fittingly titled *A Forgotten Voice: A Biography of Leta Stetter Hollingsworth* (Klein, 2002).

It is, to me, richly satisfying that it was Farrell and her friend, mentor, and Teachers College collaborator, Leta Hollingsworth (Hollingsworth dedicated *The Psychology of the Subnormal* to Farrell in recognition of her pioneering work in establishing ungraded classes), who initiated activities that eventually culminated in the establishment of the International Council for Exceptional Children. I have had the privilege of working with colleagues at Teachers College over the years, and have seen in its historic hallways of Thorndike Hall the plaque bearing Farrell's likeness in recognition of her efforts in founding CEC. That recognition aside, Farrell's role in establishing not only our organization but, to large measure, our field, is grossly underappreciated. She deserves credit, I think, for founding the notion of interdisciplinary assessment with the establishment of the psycho-educational clinic within the New York City schools, and yet the person who gets that credit, by and large, is J. E. Wallace Wallin, after whom CEC's lifetime achievement award is named. Wallin was one of the "intelligence men," in that he was an early and important voice in cautioning the use of intelligence testing too broadly, and, eventually, in establishing psycho-education clinics in schools across the country.

I have on my shelf a collection of books that date back as far as I can find with regard to the education of students with disabilities. Their titles reflect the era: *Simple Beginnings in the Training of Mentally Defective*

Children (MacDowall, 1919); *Handbook of Suggestions and Course of Study for Subnormal Children* (Holmes, 1926); *The Education of Mentally Defective Children* (Descoeudres, 1928); *Teaching Dull and Retarded Children* (Inskeep, 1929); *Education of The Slow Learning Child* (Ingram, 1935). The first name of their authors reflect the debt our field owes to women: Margaret, Mossie, Alice, Annie, Christine.

Shortly before she passed away at the age of 62, Elizabeth Farrell was feted at a luncheon honoring the 25th anniversary of her work with children in ungraded classes. I doubt she could have envisioned that the association she founded and became the first president of would become the world's largest and most influential association for special education and special educators. It's satisfying that she did, at least, live long enough to receive some recognition for her pioneering efforts. The publication of the first edition of *Elizabeth Farrell and the History of Special Education* in 2002 was a long overdue contribution to Farrell's legacy and to the debt we, as a field, owe to not only her, but to women like Leta Hollingsworth and Margaret MacDowell and Mossie Holmes and Annie Inskeep. This revised edition will continue to remind us of that debt.

So, I close with a simple proposal. I appreciate the contributions that J. E. Wallace Wallin made to our field, but it is time to rename CEC's lifetime achievement award—which recognizes an individual who has made continued and sustained contributions to the education of children and youth with exceptionalities—the Elizabeth E. Farrell Lifetime Achievement Award.

Michael L. Wehmeyer
University of Kansas

References

Adams, A. G. (1990). *An illustrated historical guide with gazetteer.* New York, NY: Fordham University Press.

American Red Cross. (1922). *Examination of pre-school age children: Examination of children upon registering before entering school.* New York, NY: Author.

Ayres, L. P. (1909). *Laggards in our schools: A study of retardation and elimination in city school systems.* New York, NY: Charities Publications Committee.

Backward child has a new chance. (1918, December 29). *The New York Times,* sec. III, p. 5.

Batterberry, M., & Batterberry, A. (1973). *On the town in New York: A history of eating, drinking, and entertainments from 1776 to the present.* New York, NY: Charles Scribner's Sons.

Board of Education of the Hendrick Hudson Central School District v. Rowley et al., 458 U.S. 175 (1982).

Brown, E. G (1905). Appendix K: A report on special classes for defective children. *Seventh annual report of the City Superintendent of Schools to the Board of Education.* New York, NY: New York City Board of Education.

Brown v. Board of Education of Topeka, 347 U.S. 483 (1954).

Carpenter, N. N. (1927). *Immigrants and their children.* U.S. Bureau of the Census Monograph No. 7. Washington, DC: U.S. Government Printing Office.

Chace, L. G. (1904, June 15–22). *Public school classes for mentally deficient children.* Presentation at the 31st National Conference of Charities and Corrections, Portland, Maine.

Coss, C. (1989). *Lillian D. Wald: Progressive activist*. New York, NY: The Feminist Press at the City University of New York.

Court Upholds Act of Miss Farrell. (1922). *Ungraded, VII*(5).

Dedication of tablet in memory of Elizabeth Farrell. (n.d.). Council for Exceptional Children Archives, Arlington, VA.

Descoeudres, A. (1928). *The education of mentally defective children: Psychological observations and practical suggestions*. London, England: George G. Harrap and Company.

Doll, E. E. (1988). Before the big time: Early history of the training school at Vineland, 1888–1949. *American Journal on Mental Retardation, 93*, 1–15.

Edson, A. W. (1921, April 1). *Subject: Report of Teachers' Council on Ungraded Classes*. Farrell Papers, Special Collections, Milbank Memorial Library, Teachers College, New York, New York.

Elizabeth E. Farrell. (1935). *Exceptional Children, 1*.

Elizabeth Farrell, noted educator of "ungraded" pupil, is buried in Utica. (1932, October 29). *The New York Times*, 5.

Fancher, R. E. (1985). *The intelligence men: Makers of the IQ controversy*. New York, NY: Norton and Company.

Farrell, E. E. (1903). Appendix F: Report on treatment of defective children in Great Britain. *Fifth annual report of the City Superintendent of Schools to the Board of Education*. New York, NY: New York City Board of Education.

Farrell, E. E. (1906–1907). Special classes in the New York City Schools. *Journal of Psychoasthenics, 11* (1–4), 91–96.

Farrell, E. E. (1907). Appendix V: Report on education of mentally defective children. *Ninth annual report of the City Superintendent of Schools to the Board of Education*. New York, NY: New York City Board of Education.

Farrell, E. E. (1908a). Appendix V: Report on education of mentally defective children. *Tenth annual report of the City Superintendent of Schools to the Board of Education*. New York, NY: New York City Board of Education.

Farrell, E. E. (1908b). The problems of the special class. *National Education Association Journal of Proceedings and Addresses of the 46th Annual Meeting* (pp. 1131–1136). Winona, MN: National Education Association.

Farrell, E. E. (1909). Appendix S: Education of mentally defective children. *Eleventh annual report of the City Superintendent of Schools to the Board of Education*. New York, NY: New York City Board of Education.

Farrell, E. E. (1910–1911). *Thirteenth annual report of the City Superintendent of Schools to the Board of Education, Ungraded classes: Report on work for mentally defective children*. New York, NY: New York City Board of Education.

Farrell, E. E. (1911–1912). *Fourteenth annual report of the City Superintendent of Schools to the Board of Education, Reports on defective children: Ungraded classes*. New York, NY: New York City Board of Education.

Farrell, E. E. (1913–1914). *Fifteenth annual report of the City Superintendent of Schools to the Board of Education, Reports on special classes: Ungraded classes*. New York, NY: New York City Board of Education.

Farrell, E. E. (1915, May). The backward child. *Ungraded, 1*(1).

Farrell, E. E. (1918–1920). *Annual report of the City Superintendent of Schools to the Board of Education, Reports on special classes: Ungraded classes*. New York, NY: New York City Board of Education.

Farrell, E. E. (1921). *Twenty-third annual report of the Superintendent of Schools to the Board of Education, Reports on special classes: Ungraded classes*. New York, NY: New York City Board of Education.

Farrell, E. E. (1923). The unclassified child. *Ungraded, VIII*(5), 97-104.

Farrell, E. E. (1924). Mental hygiene problems of maladjusted children. *Ungraded IX*(5), 99–108.

Farrell, E. E. (1925). What New York City does for its problem children. *Ungraded XI*(5), 10–18.

Farrell, E. E. (1927, July 10). Aiding the backward child. *The New York Times*, sec. VII, 7.

Farrell, E. E. (1930, February). *The present outlook*. Closing comments at the eighth annual meeting of the International Council for Exceptional Children. Council for Exceptional Children archives, Arlington, Virginia.

Goddard, H. H. (1912). *Report on the educational aspects of the public school system of the City of New York to the Committee of School Inquiry of the Board of Estimates and Apportionment: Ungraded classes*. New York, NY: New York City Board of Education.

Gullick. L. H., & Ayres, L. P. (1908). *Tenth annual report of the City Superintendent of Schools to the Board of Education, Appendix S: Causes of retardation of pupils, An investigation of retardation of fifteen schools in New York City, Borough of Manhattan.* New York, NY: New York City Board of Education.

Hollingsworth, L. S. (1920). *The psychology of the subnormal.* New York, NY: The MacMillan Company.

Hollingsworth, L. S. (1928). *The psychology of the adolescent.* New York, NY: Appleton Century.

Holmes, M. D. (1926). *Handbook of suggestions and course of study for subnormal children.* Mountain Lake Park, MD: National Publishing Society.

Ingram, C. P. (1935). *Education of the slow-learning child.* Yonkers-on-Hudson, NY: World Book Company.

Inskeep, A. D. (1929). *Teaching dull and retarded children.* New York, NY: The MacMillan Company.

Kirk, S. A., & Lord, F. E. (Eds.) (1974). *Exceptional children: Educational resources and perspectives.* Boston, MA: Houghton-Mifflin.

Klein, A. G. (2002). *A forgotten voice: A biography of Leta Stetter Hollingsworth.* Scottsdale, AZ: Great Potential Press.

Kode, K. (2002). *Elizabeth Farrell and the history of special education.* Arlington, VA: Council for Exceptional Children.

Kode, K. E. (2001). *Guarding the sacred fires: Elizabeth E. Farrell's contributions to the creation of special education in New York City* (Doctoral dissertation). Proquest Digital Dissertations Paper AAI3049933. http://epublications.marquette.edu/dissertations/AAI3049933

Krishef, C. H. (1983). *An introduction to mental retardation.* Springfield, IL: Charles C Thomas.

Link, A. S., & McCormick, R. L. (1983). *Progressivism.* Arlington Heights, IL: Harlan Davidson.

Longstreet, S. (1975.) *City on two rivers: Profiles on New York—Yesterday and today.* New York, NY: Hawthorn Books.

MacDowall, M. (1919). *Simple beginnings in the training of mentally defective children.* London, England: Local Government Press.

Marcellus, New York. (1865). *Town of Marcellus Census.*

Maxwell, W. H. (1899). *First annual report of the City Superintendent of Schools to the Board of Education.* New York, NY: New York City Board of Education.

Maxwell, W. H. (1902). *Fourth annual report of the City Superintendent of Schools to the Board of Education.* New York, NY: New York City Board of Education.

Maxwell, W. H. (1905). *Seventh annual report of the City Superintendent of Schools to the Board of Education.* New York, NY: New York City Board of Education.

Maxwell, W. H. (1906). *Eighth annual report of the City Superintendent of Schools to the Board of Education.* New York, NY: New York City Board of Education.

Maxwell, W. H. (1910). *Twelfth annual report of the City Superintendent of Schools to the Board of Education.* New York, NY: New York City Board of Education.

McCarthy, D. (1956). *History of the New York State Psychological Association.* Unpublished manuscript.

Memorial resolutions. (1932, November 28). Farrell Papers, Special Collections, Milbank Memorial Library, Teachers College, New York City, New York.

Mills v. Board of Education of the District of Columbia, 348 F. Supp. 866 (D.D.C. 1972).

Minutes of the eleventh Annual Meeting of the International Council for the Education of Exceptional Children. (1933). Council for Exceptional Children Archives, Arlington, VA.

Notes and news. (1921). *The Psychological Bulletin, 18,* 439.

O'Shea, W. J. (1926). *Twenty-eighth annual report of City Superintendent of Schools to the Board of Education.* New York, NY: New York City Board of Education.

PARC v. Commonwealth of Pennsylvania, 343 F. Supp. 279; U.S. Dist. LEXIS 13874 (1972).

Peter, L. J. (1977). *Peter's quotations: Ideas for our time.* New York, NY: Quill.

Rice, J. M. (1893). *The public school system of the United States.* New York, NY: Century.

Safford, P. L., & Safford, E. J. (1996). *A history of childhood and disability.* New York, NY: Teachers College Press.

Sarason, S. B., & Doris, J. (1979). *Educational handicap, public policy and social history.* New York, NY: The Free Press.

Siegel, B. (1983). *Lillian Wald of Henry Street.* New York, NY: Macmillan.

Smith, J. D., & Wehmeyer, M. L. (2012). *Good blood, bad blood: Science, nature, and the myth of the Kallikaks.* Washington DC: American Association on Intellectual and Developmental Disabilities.

Stevens, E. L. (1903). *Fifth annual report of the City Superintendent of Schools to the Board of Education.* New York, NY: New York City Board of Education.

Superintendent Maxwell plans more school novelties. (1906, March 4). *The New York Times,* 20.

Teachers Council Report of Committee on Special Schools and Classes. Re: Place of ungraded child in the public school system. (1920, November 5). Farrell Papers, Special Collections, Milbank Memorial Library, Teachers College, New York, NY.

Trattner, W. I. (1999). *From poor law to welfare state: A history of social welfare in America* (6th ed.). New York, NY: The Free Press.

Ungraded classes mark 25th year. (1932, March 6). *The New York Times,* 13.

United Neighborhood Houses. (n.d.). *Settlement house history.* Retrieved from http://www.unhny.org/about/history

Wald, L. D. (1915). *The house on Henry Street.* New York, NY: Henry Holt & Co.

Wald, L. D. (1941). *Windows on Henry Street.* Boston, MA: Little, Brown, & Co.

Warner, L. (n.d.). *Founders of the International Council for Exceptional Children.* Unpublished article. Council for Exceptional Children Archives, Arlington, VA.

Warner, L. (1922, August 10). *Minutes of the organization of the Council for the Education of Exceptional Children* [meeting minutes].

Warner, L. (1942). Early history of the International Council for Exceptional Children, *Journal of Exceptional Children, 8,* 245.

William H. Maxwell to Jacob W. Mack (May 12, 1903). Farrell Papers, Special Collections, Milbank Memorial Library, Teachers College, New York.

Wooden, H. Z. (1962, March 30). [Letter to Mary E. Harnett]. Council for Exceptional Children Archives, Arlington, VA.

Yans-McLaughlin, V., & Lightman, M. (1997). *Ellis Island and the peopling of America: The official guide.* New York, NY: The New Press.

Zenderland, L. (1998). *Measuring minds: Henry Herbert Goddard and the origins of American intelligence testing.* New York, NY: Cambridge University Press.

Appendix

Minutes of the Organizational Meeting, August 1922

Minutes of the Organization of the
Council for the Education of
Exceptional Children

On August 10, 1922, a group of people interested in Education for all types of Special Children met together at a dinner conference in New York City for the pupose of organizing an association of Special Class education.

The business meeting was opened by Miss Elizabeth E. Farrell, Inspector of Ungradeed Classes, N.Y.C., who acted as chairman.

The first order of business was the election of officers.

Miss Alice C Smithick, conductor of Psychological Tests, Montclair, New Jersey, nominated Miss Farrell for president. The nominations were moved to be closed, seconded and carried and Miss Farrell was unanimously elected President

Miss La Vinia Warner, Director of Special Education, Ohio University, Athens, Ohio, was nominated secretary by Miss Harriette A. Johnson, Supervisor of Special Education, Oakland, California. The nominations were closed, seconded and carried.

Miss Jessie B. Doring, Assistant Supervisor of Ungraded classes, N.Y.C. was elected Vice-President and Miss Estella McCafferty, Principal of Jackson Opportunity School, Kansas City, was elected treasurer.

The President then asked for suggestions for a name for the new organization. Several names were given and discussed. The name of <u>Interational Council for the Education of Exceptional Children</u>, was propsed by Miss Jennie L. Dall, Superintendent of Girl's Vocational School, Aligarh, India. It was moved by Miss Smithick that this name be adopted. The motion was carried.

It was voted that the International Council for the Education of Exceptional Children hold its First Annual Meeting in February, 1923, at the same time and place that the Dept. of Superintendence of National Education Association holds its meeting.

The question of membership was then announced by the President. It was moved that the membership include any person who was interested in the Education of Exceptional Children

The next order of business was that of membership fees. It was moved by Miss Imegene Palen, Teacher of Lip Reading, Toronto, Canada that the fee for one year be $1.00 The motion was carried.

A motion was then made by Miss Johnson that there be one grade of membership, active. The motion wa carried.